NAPOLEON

Napoleon

David G. Chandler

LEO COOPER

For my three sons
Paul, John and Mark

First Published in 1973 by
Weidenfeld and Nicolson Limited

Published in this format in 2001 by

Leo Cooper,
an imprint of
Pen & Sword Books Ltd.,
47 Church Street, Barnsley,
South Yorkshire.
S70 2AS

A CIP record for this book is available from the British Library

ISBN: 0-85052-750-3

Printed in Great Britain by
C P I UK

CONTENTS

Introduction

This book is about one of the most remarkable military leaders in the history of war. Drawing up lists of the great commanders is a highly subjective occupation. There is room for more that one opinion about the qualifications of Tamurlane, Wellington or Mao Tse-Tung. Some great battlefield commanders had only the shakiest grasp of grand strategy; and some of the most brilliant staff officers would have been hard put to it to command a troop of boy scouts on a bird-watching patrol. But no serious military historian would contest the claim of Napoleon Bonaparte to a pre-eminent place in the soldier's pantheon. Indeed, one contemporary British general has declared with definitive candour 'There have been only three great commanders in history: Alexander the Great, Napoleon and myself.'

If a historical novelist were to invent such a character, he would be accused of fantasy. Born into a poor Corsican family of ancient lineage, Napoleon Bonaparte went to school in France at the age of eight. When he was fifteen he went to L' École Militaire in Paris. Ten years later he was a General commanding the French Army of the interior; and at the age of thirty-five he was crowned Emperor of France. At his side was his Empress, Josephine, the beautiful widow of a French aristocrat. Such things do not happen to ordinary men; and it is illuminating to analyse the qualities which lifted Napoleon so rapidly and so spectacularly to the commanding heights of power.

A study of the careers of great military leaders reveals the notably unsurprising fact that they are all different. They are fat and thin, graceless and elegant, practical and imaginative, sensitive and crude. Both Genghis Khan and Ulysees Grant were great leaders; but it is difficult to imagine that they had much else in common. Yet it is possible to identify a number of qualities which emerge again and again in any analysis of the characters of successful military commanders. They include single-mindedness, ruthlessness, a remarkable capacity for sustained hard work, and above all that strange, indefinable magnetism of personality which is nowadays described, inaccurately but vividly, as charisma. Some great leaders got by with only one of these qualities; some possessed two or more in varying degrees. Napoleon had them all. To study his life and his campaigns is something like watching the operation of a computer programmed for relentless success as a leader. If you press the button marked Man Management or Human Relations, out comes the Little Corporal, moving among the veteran troops whom he called his children, using his phenomenal memory to address them each by name. Indicate Single-Mindedness and there appears the image of General Bonaparte deciding dispassionately that it was more important for him to be in Paris in the autumn of 1799, furthering his own ambitious plans, than to be conducting abortive military operations in Egypt. He therefore quite simply went home, handing over his Army to an enraged subordinate. No one who has read the story of the operations in Egypt and Syria would doubt his ruthlessness when, after the fall of Jaffa on 7 March 1799, five thousand prisoners were slaughtered on the pretext that they had broken parole. His capacity for work was phenomenal - he apparently made do with four or five hours' sleep each day and was capable of dictating simultaneously to several secretaries, changing constantly from one subject to another without losing his train of thought in any of them. In the matter of charisma, it would seem churlish to doubt the powers of a man who, in spite of a somewhat unpromising physical appearance, succeeded in enchanting successively Josephine de Beauharnais, Marie Walewska and Marie Louise, daughter of the Emperor of Austria; but it was not only women who were captivated by Napoleon.

Napoleon, as is often the fate of giants, has been the target of constant attack by pygmies. It has been suggested that he suffered from hysteria, epilepsy, satyriasis, piles and sundry other ailments. He has been accused of insensitivity, bad manners and vindictive cruelty - and it has to be conceded that he was often guilty of all these. But no one who knows the history of war has ever denied that he was a military genius and peerless leader of men. His place in history is secure and the story of his life makes irresistible reading.

Lord Chalfont

Preface

Napoleon Bonaparte must be regarded as the pre-eminent soldier of modern history. He must be placed among the four greatest commanders of all time, sharing the foremost honours in the Halls of Valhalla with Alexander the Great, Hannibal and Genghis Khan. For nigh on twenty years he was virtually unchallengable as a strategist and grand tactician, and for half that spell he was in effect the arbiter of the Fate of Europe and the dominant personality on the world scene. Here was a genius - and the fact that he was ultimately condemned to die an exiled captive does not materially detract from his greatness.

In the years of his prime, Napoleon's abilities in both the military and the civil fields were unsurpassed. Massive legal and administrative achievements balance to a considerable extent the several million deaths and incalculable misery caused by the long series of wars inevitably associated with his name. More than any other man, he left an indelible print on Europe, ushering in the modern nationalistic age which is only slowly giving place today to international co-operation and schemes of union - a concept of which Napoleon, too, had dreamed in his greatest years. More than any other soldier since the invention of firearms, he revolutionised the conduct of warfare, replacing the outdated eighteenth-century concepts of siege and stately manoeuvre with a form of blitzkrieg, conducted over a dozen campaigns and resulting in some sixty battles, which has dominated warfare down to the present day. Even if modern preoccupations with nuclear stalemate and the problems of guerrilla or revolutionary struggles have somewhat dimmed the significance of large field armies and challenged the all-importance of the major battles, Napoleon's contribution to the art of war remains central and relevant.

Nevertheless, his eclipse was thoroughly deserved - there were decided limits to his greatness, and later years brought out the perversions of the qualities that first marked him out from among his fellow men. He was, to borrow Clarendon's description of Cromwell, '... a great, bad man.' He became a tyrant and a bully, the victim of his own propaganda; he proved unwilling to adjust his military concepts (or incapable of doing so), even when it became clear that his enemies had devised viable responses to his strategic machinations; he came to mistrust his closest associates, and continually grumbled about their lack of initiative and skill, yet refused either to replace them or to provide them with training in the higher realms of the art of war; he closed his mind to reality, refusing to admit the gravity of the continuous conflict in Spain while proposing to launch half a million men against Russia - some fifteen hundred miles dividing the two theatres of war; he underestimated the impact of guerrilla operations, scorned Great Britain's implacable hostility and never came to grips with the fundamentals of naval warfare. Nevertheless, even when all this has been said, he remained a dynamic commander, the foremost soldier in Europe. That it is possible to claim this equally of the years of his decline gives some indication of his phenomenal qualities in the years of his prime. Here was no common mortal.

My aim in writing this book originally was to afford the opportunity of studying this great subject to the general reader for whom my earlier work, *The Campaigns of Napoleon,* was probably a trifle too daunting in size and scope. It is interesting to note that this latter book is now in its nineteenth edition. I am delighted that *Napoleon* is being reborn under Leo Cooper/Pen and Sword imprint. My thanks go to Charles Hewitt and Brigadier Henry Wilson for taking up the challenge.

As before, I am grateful to my original publishers, the MacMillan Company of New York, for permission to cite parts of *The Campaigns of Napoleon* and to Colonel Tom Greiss of the Department of History, United States Military Academy, West Point for the reproduction of battle sketch diagrams.

Finally I hope that readers of all ages will enjoy this book about a giant of a man whose reputation is surely unrivalled.

Vive l'Empereur

D.G.C.
Yateley, Hampshire,
December 2000

Dr David G. Chandler

Educated at Keble College, Oxford, Dr David G. Chandler served in the British Army for four years. He taught at the Royal Military Academy Sandhurst for over 33 years becoming Head of the War Studies Department (1980-1994). His other appointments have included Visiting Professor of Ohio State University, the Virginia Military Institute and the US Marine Corps University, Quantico, and Trustee of the Royal Armouries. He is also Honorary President of the British Commission for Military History, Fellow of the Royal Historical Society and was made D.Litt. at Oxford University in 1991.

One of the world's leading authorities on his period, Dr Chandler's many published works include the acclaimed *The Campaigns of Napoleon; The Dictionary of the Napoleonic Wars; Waterloo – The Hundred Days* and, of course, *Napoleon,* which Pen & Sword Books Ltd. are delighted to republish under their Leo Cooper Imprint.

CHAPTER ONE

Preparation and Promise
1769-95

'I have a presentiment that one day this small island will astonish Europe', wrote Jean-Jacques Rousseau of Corsica in 1762. It was a time at which Corsica's struggle for independence under her leader General Paoli had captured the romantic imagination of liberals everywhere. Of less obvious significance, Paoli numbered among his lieutenants a cultured, kindly, if not particularly notable, Corsican called Carlo Buonaparte.

The first signs of leadership: the young Napoleone Buonaparte leaves his books aside at Brienne to lead his comrades in a snowball fight.

Corsica, and Buonaparte, did indeed astonish Europe, though in a way hardly to be foreseen even by the prophetic Rousseau. Just seven years after this famous prediction, Paoli was defeated by the French, and Corsica's dream of independence destroyed; but in August that year, 1769, Carlo's wife Letizia gave birth to a son, Napoleon, who was to become not just an outstanding soldier, nor just a great leader, but one of the most successful conquerors known to history.

Napoleon was not to suffer for his family's association with the Corsican rebel. On the contrary, the influential Baron Marboeuf, a close friend of Carlo and Letizia, was able to secure places for both Napoleon and his elder brother Joseph at Brienne, a royal school founded by the French king's Minister of War, St Germain, for the sons of the nobility. It was not easy to prove - as

The Buonaparte family arms, as registered in 1779. Proof of nobility was vital to gain Napoleon a place at Brienne.

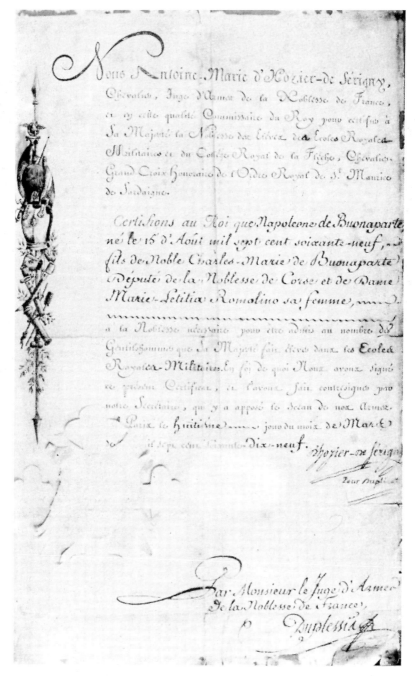

The certificate of nobility necessary for Napoleone's entry at Brienne, issued at Paris, 18 March 1779.

was necessary - that the Buonapartes had descended from generations of nobility, for although they were an old and prominent Corsican family - with an Italian lineage which could be traced back to the eleventh century - they were scarcely noble in the contemporary sense. However, the formalities were eventually completed and, at the age of nine, Napoleon left the land of his birth for the wider horizon of France.

The first step was a preliminary year at a college at Autun, at which the brothers put a little polish on their spoken and written French; then Brienne, where Napoleon spent five and a half years. It was a time of mixed emotions. As a child, the quietly-spoken, impoverished and intensely proud Corsican suffered from both loneliness and homesickness, thinking often of his mother, whom he adored, and his growing family of brothers and sisters of whom Lucien, Eliza, Louis, Pauline, Caroline and Jerome - apart from Joseph - survived beyond infancy. At school he was mocked and mimicked by his fellows, and was doubtless developing that

Letizia Buonaparte (1750-1836), 'Madame Mére'. Always a realist, her favourite phrase during her family's advancement was 'So long as it lasts.'

sense of being different, of uniqueness, which was to drive him onwards throughout his career as a man of destiny.

But Napoleon's schooldays were not unsuccessful. He began to show his precocious talent for leadership, organising elaborate war-games and, one hard winter, a snowball fight of heroic and not altogether bloodless proportions in which his juniors outclassed the seniors. He also applied himself to his studies, showing particular promise in mathematics. Towards the end of his schooling, a royal inspector wrote the following report: 'Height - five feet three inches. Constitution - excellent health, docile expression, mild, straightforward, thoughtful. Conduct - most satisfactory: has always been distinguished for his application in mathematics. He is fairly well acquainted with history and geography. He is weak in all accomplishments - drawing, dancing, music and the like. This boy would make an excellent sailor; deserves to be admitted to the school in Paris.' He was not, however, destined for a nautical career. His ambition was already set on a commission in the artillery.

The place was duly secured, and in late October 1784, he joined L'École Militaire in Paris. His formal training lasted less than a year, for in the spring of 1785 his father died, and this was both a great personal loss and a major crisis for the bereaved family. Brothers Joseph and Lucien returned home to aid their mother, but Napoleon stayed on to complete his training. He was probably allowed to pass-out well ahead of his time for compassionate reasons; he was placed only fifty-fifth, but at least he was receiving a pittance of pay from 31 October 1785, no small part of it being transmitted back to Corsica to assist his family. And so it was that probationer *sous-lieutenant* Buonaparte joined the La Fére Artillery Regiment at Valence on 5 November 1785. The greatest military career in history had begun.

It was a propitious, if dangerous, moment. French government and society were heaving under the strains which would shortly dissolve the nation - and Europe - in the tumult of the Revolution. With the Revolution would come internal chaos and external threat which would provide opportunities for both political leadership and strong generalship; alternatively, ambitions could just as easily lead to the guillotine. Moreover, the egalitarian nature of the Revolution would provide chances for men of lower birth rather than for the traditional French nobility who had hitherto dominated in Church and State. More practically, Napoleon began his career at a time at which, technically, the French army was potentially equipped for the successes which Napoleon was to achieve. Out of the disasters of the Seven Years War in mid-century had come new energy and application to modernise her weapons, particularly in the fields of artillery. The great Gribeauval had played a leading role in these developments, and it would not be long before French armies, and her generals, would reap the reward.

It is therefore significant that young Napoleon began his service by learning in fullest detail the profession of a gunner. He learned how to handle rammer and shot, to sight a gun and to command a detachment. When he had mastered these things, his commission was confirmed and, modestly enough, he saw his first active service in quelling local food riots at Lyons.

Portrait of Bonaparte soon after the establishment of his reputation, c. 1797. Sketch by David.

Portrait of Josephine as Empress, detail from painting by Lefebvre at La Malmaison.

L'École Militaire, Paris, where the young Buonaparte, aged 15, spent a year under officer training. The print shows a parade of a later date.

Soon it was time for his first leave, which, by one means and another, he managed to extend from February 1787 to June 1788. No doubt he found garrison duty boring, but it is indicative of the easy-going nature of the Bourbon authorities that they would countenance such lengthy absences. Indeed, his first six years as an officer would include no less than thirty-two months on leave. During his first return to Corsica, the ambitious youth started to write a history of the island. He was still inspired with the goal of Corsican independence and looked upon Paoli, now in exile, as a hero. It was an admiration which would not last much longer.

Following his return to duty, Napoleon spent an important and formative year. He was posted to Auxonne, where he was appointed secretary to a board of senior artillery officers conducting experiments with cannon and shells. This brought him into close touch with the best artillerists of the day, and above all with Baron du Teil, one of Gribeauval's disciples, who took the keen young officer under his wing. The Commandant lent Napoleon many books, encouraging him to study the wider spectrum of warfare, and stage by stage he began to gather those ideas of strategic and grand tactical manoeuvre from works of history and military affairs which were to form the basis of his generalship. As we shall see later, Napoleon was not an original thinker where military theory was concerned; his genius was wholly practical - he made other men's concepts work and improved upon them: hence the importance of these months at Auxonne, during which the foundations of future greatness were

Cadet Napoleone Buonaparte - the earliest known sketch from life, 1785.

indubitably laid. He was an avid reader and an apt pupil, and absorbed all that the Baron could provide.

The winter of 1788 saw Napoleon seriously ill - possibly due to an inadequate diet, as he sought to save more money for transmission to his family. He recovered, and the following September, as the first waves of the Revolution swept across France, he set out again for Corsica on leave, and plunged into the local ferment. Paoli had returned to Corsica in triumph, and Napoleon, now an ardent revolutionary, saw his hero's patriotism as perfectly compatible with the ideals of the Revolution. He involved himself in local politics, exploiting a new regulation passed by the National Assembly which permitted regular officers to hold additional, elected, ranks in the volunteer battalions being raised in various areas. On 1 April 1792, Napoleon duly became Lieutenant-Colonel of the Ajaccio Volunteers, assuring his election by the simple, if unscrupulous, method of arranging for his fellow-candidates to be kidnapped for the period of election day. But the rift with Paoli had come. Paoli was no revolutionary, but royalist and, in the conflict, pro-British. Napoleon earned his hostility both by his severe repression of local rioting and by his support of a French investigation into Corsican affairs. The Buonaparte family had to flee Corsica to escape from Paoli's vengeance and, in June 1793, settled near Marseilles. As for Corsica, it was surrendered to the British who held it for three years.

For the Buonaparte family, for France and for Europe, 1793 was

A cartoon by Cruikshank: 'Napoleon working the gun at Toulon'. His achievements at the siege in 1793 first made his name known, and earned him promotion to Brigadier-General.

indeed a critical year. By now the Revolution was entering its bloodiest phase. Louis xvi and his Queen, Marie Antoinette had been executed. The new French Republic, torn with internal dissension, was at war with almost the whole of Europe, the fruit of their absurd boast that they would help 'all peoples who rise against their rulers'. The Austrian Empire, with its extensive possessions from eastern Europe to Italy, had entered the lists. So too had England, with her command of the seas. Meanwhile, France herself was torn by rebellion in various provinces, and this gave Napoleon his first great chance - the operation at Toulon.

Toulon, an important naval base, had defected from the Republic and admitted an Allied force under Admiral Lord Hood, and thus

caused a major crisis for the Revolutionary government, currently headed by 'the Dictator', Maximilien Robespierre, and the Committee of Public Safety. The first efforts to regain the town were highly ineffectual, but then fate took a hand by directing Captain Buonaparte past the scene immediately after the army's senior gunner had been wounded. He at once suggested himself for the vacancy, and *faute pour mieux* found his offer accepted by General Carteaux.

This was not quite so miraculous an opportunity as might at first sight appear. Several weeks earlier, to fill an idle day or two, Napoleon had written a political tract, *Le Souper de Beaucaire,* which had found its way to Augustin Robespierre, brother of 'the Dictator' and currently an all-important Representative of the People (or political commissar) in the south of France. The revolutionary tone of this pamphlet impressed Augustin, and it was a fellow Representative, Salicetti, who used the vast powers of his office to induce Carteaux to accept Bonaparte for the vacancy. He thus secured the post more on political than on military grounds.

With vast energy and determination, the young officer devoted his attention to the siege of Toulon. Backed as he was by the all-powerful Representatives, whose word was literally law, he forced through his ideas no matter what the opposition of his normal superiors. Promoted *chef de bataillon* (major) on 18 October, Buonaparte intrigued for (and secured) the removal of Carteaux's successor from the senior command, and by mid-November he had persuaded the next general, Dugommier, that his plan was correct. His military appreciation of the situation convinced him that the key to Toulon lay in capturing the fort protecting Point l'Eguilette, a promontory commanding the outer harbour. Its possession would make it impossible for Hood's fleet to stay in the inner anchorage, and if the fleet left, the city must fall. On 17 December, after weeks of careful preparation, the assault went in; within a few hours, Fort Mulgrave was in French hands, and before the day was out l'Eguilette was taken - Major Bonaparte receiving a slight wound in the thigh during the fighting. His intuition proved

Imprisoned on suspicion of treason after the fall of Robespierre, General Bonaparte continued his military studies even under the shadow of the guillotine in the Fort d' Antibes, 1794.

correct. Within a day Lord Hood had gone, and on the 19th Toulon was reoccupied by the French forces.

As a reward for his services, the Representatives promoted Bonaparte to Brigadier-General on 22 December. He was a little over twenty-four years old. Napoleon's success in Toulon stamped him as a promising young soldier of outstanding qualities - qualities sorely needed by the authorities in Paris. The road to preferment seemed open and inviting before him. Under the patronage of Augustin Robespierre and Salicetti, he became senior gunner to General Dumerbion's army in Italy, the most important sphere of operations against the Austrians. It was due largely to Napoleon's meticulous planning that the French captured both Loano, in April 1794, and the area known as 'the Barricades'.

Shortly afterwards, Napoleon went on an intelligence mission to Genoa, an episode which nearly cost him his head, for in the troubled world of Revolutionary France even success could prove its own undoing. In July a *coup d'état* swept Robespierre and the Jacobin faction from power, all his closest supporters being rounded up by the new regime, the Directory. Napoleon was among those arrested, and he was shut up in the Fort d'Antibes on a trumped-up charge of treasonable behaviour in Genoa. His imprisonment lasted only a fortnight, for his skills were needed by the hard-pressed army in Italy, but in the months which followed his release, he was alternately dismissed and re-instated as the political pendulum swung in Paris. At times he despaired, contemplating leaving France altogether and placing his sword at the disposal of the Sultan of Turkey. Then, at the beginning of October 1795, came a decisive moment. The Paris mob, in one of its periodic fits of revolt, rose against the Directory. Paul Barras, one of

A cartoon by Gillray: British propaganda showing the ardent young general surprising his wife-to-be and Mme Tallien dancing naked before the lecherous Barras. The caption alleges that Bonaparte earned promotion by taking Josephine off the hands of Barras.

the Directors, was charged with organising a defence, and he turned to ex-Brigadier-General Bonaparte, asking him to take the necessary measures. Napoleon did not hesitate. Sending Captain Murat, with whom he had fought in Italy, to secure some guns, he drew up his dispositions to isolate the Tuilleries Palace where the mob would make its attempted *coup*. When, on 5 October, the anticipated attack took place, the rioters, surging forward, were met with salvoes from cannon at point blank range. Two hundred died instantly; the 'whiff of grapeshot' succeeded in crushing the revolt; and the events of 13 *Vendémiaire* made Napoleon's fortune. Praise and rewards were lavished on him by a grateful Directory. By 16 October he had been promoted *Général de Division;* ten days later he was appointed to command the Army of the Interior.

This astonishing rise had taken Napoleon, at twenty-six, to a pinnacle of professional achievement. At the same time, he began to contemplate a change of a more personal nature, for in the aftermath of *Vendémiaire* the Paris citizens were ordered to surrender their weapons to the government, and Napoleon was visited by a fourteen-year-old boy, Eugène, who pleaded that his mother might keep her late husband's sword. The General acceded, and was visited by the widow herself, Josephine de Beauharnais, who wanted to thank him personally. She was six years older than Napoleon, still very beautiful, with an aristocratic background which had once brought her to the verge of execution before Robespierre's fall had saved her. Napoleon fell passionately in love. Josephine, a former mistress of Barras, now became mistress to the victor of *Vendémiaire.* A few months later, on 9 March 1796, they were married.

The honeymoon lasted two days. Already Napoleon had laid plans for his next command, daily bombarding the Ministry with criticism and advice concerning the feeble campaign being waged in Italy. In the month of his marriage, he was given the appointment he wanted, supreme command in Italy. On the 26th he arrived in Nice with his specially-appointed staff, which included Alexandre Berthier at its head and Colonel Murat as senior *aide de camp.* So far, Napoleon's success had resulted largely from good fortune. He had never directed a large-scale military operation. He had studied hard, thought a great deal and was confident in his abilities. Now these abilities would be tested, and Napoleon, and the world, would discover whether the precocious careerist was in fact a military commander of the first rank.

CHAPTER TWO

Italy, Egypt and Brumaire
1796-99

In Italy, General Bonaparte (as his name now became, in the French form) found himself commanding a neglected, ill-disciplined and largely demoralised force of some 37,600 men. They were hemmed in along the narrow Ligurian Plain by the forces of Austria, under General Beaulieu, and their allies - albeit reluctant ones - the Piedmontese under General Colli, who were holding the mountains from Cuneo to the vicinity of Voltri; while the Royal Navy dominated the Gulf of Genoa. It was a situation to daunt the most optimistic soldier. Napoleon's divisional generals, Massena, Augereau and Sérurier, treated their new commander with barely-concealed amusement; the troops badly needed a victory and they needed to extricate themselves from their precarious position. Napoleon's solution involved a strategy which was to characterise some of his later campaigns: to concentrate against the centre of a widely-deployed enemy and defeat them piecemeal by a concentration of forces at one particular point. In this instance, knowing that his army must starve and disintegrate if it remained in its present position, Bonaparte planned to break through into the fertile plains of Piedmont without delay, as a preliminary to the conquest of the Milanese, his strategic objective.

A surprise move by the Austrians towards Savona and Voltri precipitated the French offensive.* Aiming to divide Colli's twenty-five thousand Piedmontese from Beaulieu's dispersed thirty-one thousand Austrians prior to defeating them in detail, Bonaparte struck north from the coast on 11 April. After repulsing a detachment of Beaulieu's army at Montenotte the next day, the main French force swung west to attack Colli, the primary target. Delays and a crisis involving Massena's division holding the right flank at Dego held Bonaparte up for three vital days, but by the 17th the advance on Ceva had been resumed, associated with a switch of the army's communications from the exposed route to the coast to the safer Col de Tende.

* See map page 175.

Napoleon, victor of Lodi, attended by the allegorical figure of Fame who is busily inscribing his martial achievements for prosperity.

Remorseless pressure brought Colli to action at Mondovi on the 22nd, and the subsequent French pursuit, pushed to the uttermost, induced Piedmont to sign the Armistice of Cherasco on the 28th. Thus seventeen days had sufficed for the elimination of one opponent; and Napoleon's 'strategy of the central position', used here for the first time, had, despite certain imperfections, proved its value.

After a pause to resupply his near-starving troops, Bonaparte swung east in an attempt to trap the bewildered Beaulieu, but the Austrians managed to elude the French and cross to the north bank of the River Po. With superior forces at his disposal (some 6,800 reinforcements had reached him from the Col de Tende), the General now set out to employ another of his theories, the 'strategy of envelopment'. Feinting with Sérurier's division towards Valenza (to distract and preoccupy Beaulieu), the main body was force-marched down the south bank of the Po to Piacenza far in the Austrian's rear, crossed the river (7-9 May) and set out to occupy the River Adda crossings so as to isolate the Austrian army from any hope of reinforcement by severing its communications with its base at Mantua.

The French, however, unused to the method, were too slow. Beaulieu realised his peril in time and retreated over the Adda precipitately, and as a result the famous battle of Lodi was fought against only his rearguard on 10 May. Bonaparte sited guns in person and helped storm the bridge, and the Austrians had decidedly the worst of the encounter. It all amounted to far less than he had hoped, but nevertheless, Lodi won him the confidence of the troops, who gave him his famous nickname, 'the little corporal'.

Five days later, the French were masters of Milan, and without pause Bonaparte hounded his men on to force the Mincio river-line near Borghetto on the 30th. The stunned Austrians promptly split their army, part retiring north up the Adige valley to Trent, the rest seeking sanctuary within the great fortress of Mantua, set amid lakes and marshes, the key to the famous 'Quadrilateral' of fortresses (Mantua, Peschiera, Verona and Legnano) guarding the Alpine pass-exits. Garrisoned by twelve thousand men with 316 cannon, Mantua, and successive Austrian attempts to relieve it, would dominate the next nine months. By 3 June it was closely besieged.

With his forces investing Mantua, Bonaparte busied himself reorganising the conquered Milanese, but the French were soon unpopular, and serious risings had to be suppressed.

To make matters worse, the Directory attached by no means the same importance to the Italian campaign as did Napoleon. Their ideas were more limited: to pick up useful territorial acquisitions which might be used as a bargaining counter in an eventual peace with Austria; to plunder its treasures for the precarious Paris Exchequer; and to create in Italy a large-scale diversion to assist the major drive against Austria which, for them, meant the planned

*Attempting to trap the Austrians, the French army siezes ferry-boats near
Piacenza on the River Po, 8 May 1796.*

offensive under Generals Moreau and Jourdan due - overdue - to
move across the Rhine and into the Danube valley. This was very
far from Napoleon's ambition to establish control over the whole of
north Italy, and hence his chilly reception of the Directory's attempt
to divide the Italian army in two, with Napoleon's command
confined in operations and plunder to the south. Napoleon hinted
at resignation, and retorted that 'One bad commander is better than
two good ones.' He won his point, and the convoys of looted art-
treasures which he sent off to Paris helped to remind doubters of his
indispensability.

   With Mantua under siege, and the Austrians' hold on north Italy
threatened, Napoleon could expect the enemy to move without
delay. General Würmser, who had replaced Beaulieu, was soon
massing an army around Trent with fresh troops released by the
failure of France's Rhine offensive to begin on schedule. In July
Würmser advanced in three columns down each side of Lake Garda
and the distant Brenta valley respectively, hoping to divide and
distract the French. Weaker than his fifty-thousand-strong

opponent in terms of a field force, Bonaparte was set the task of intercepting, and defeating, each force in turn without allowing one to reach Mantua. This proved beyond his capacity, and he was soon talking about taking 'serious measures for a defeat'. To gain men for battle, he was compelled to order Sérurier's division to abandon the siege of Mantua. On 3 August Bonaparte rushed twenty thousand men to beat back the westernmost column at First Lonato, but this enabled Würmser to slip troops into Mantua from the east. Fortunately, the Austrian general was slow to move towards the main French army - Augereau fighting a staunch delaying action to win Bonaparte a little time. Making use of this, the French countermarched from Lonato, and on 5 August were able to face Würmser's twenty-five thousand men with twenty-eight thousand at Castiglione. Sérurier's division from Mantua came up a trifle early against the Austrian left and rear, and as a result Würmser was able to extricate some twenty thousand men and head back towards Trent up the Adige valley. The French had driven off the first Austrian relief army, but not before it had resupplied Mantua - and, on 10 August, the siege had to be started all over again.

Meanwhile, away on the Rhine, Jourdan's belated offensive had run into difficulties, but by mid-August Moreau was making substantial progress on the Danube front. The Directory thereupon ordered the Army of Italy to mount a major diversion towards Trent and the Tyrol, despite the complication of an untamed Mantua in its rear. Bonaparte therefore advanced with thirty-three thousand men up the Adige valley to test the Austrian hold on the Tyrol, but Würmser was in fact already on the move southwards. Leaving only fourteen thousand men around Trent, he led twenty thousand down the Brenta valley, his aim once again being to relieve Mantua and challenge the French hold on the Milanese.

As soon as he realised the new situation, Bonaparte abandoned his Tyrol scheme, left General Vaubois with ten thousand men to

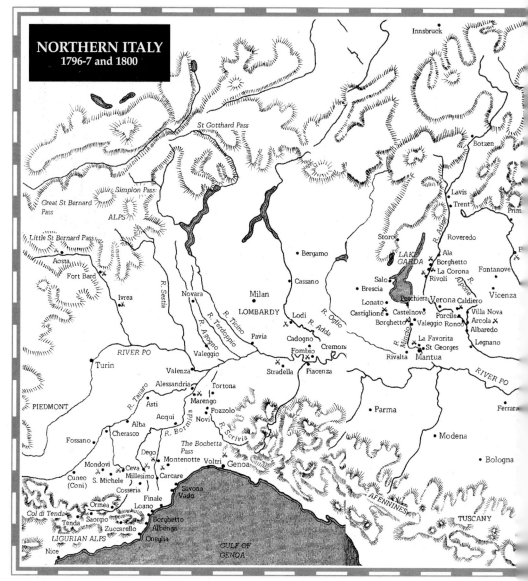

NORTHERN ITALY
1796-7 and 1800

face Trent and rushed the rest down the Brenta valley behind his adversary. He caught and soundly beat Würmser at Bassano on 8 September, and the Austrians were forced to split up, part heading east for Trieste, part (with Würmser) making for Mantua, where they succeeded in breaking through the siege lines on the 12th to raise the garrison's strength to all of twenty-three thousand men.

The French reimposed the siege next day, but were no nearer to capturing the great fortress than they had been in June. Another temporary lull settled over the theatre of war, during which Bonaparte busied himself in creating three new republics to

consolidate his grip on his conquests. But the French remained just as unpopular with the local people.

By October, Moreau's Danube offensive, which, after all, Bonaparte had been able to do little to assist, was on the verge of collapse, and this enabled Vienna to find more men for Italy. General Alvintzi, a new Austrian commander appointed with Würmser out of action in Mantua, had soon built up an army of forty-six thousand, and leaving eighteen thousand of these to lure the French towards Trent, he marched the remainder through Bassano, and headed for Verona,

The Austrian general, Count Würmser, who made attempts to relieve Mantua but ended up being incarcerated there himself.

the very linchpin of the French defence arrangements, pushing Massena's division before him. Simultaneously, The Austrians applied remorseless pressure to Vaubois, who also gave ground. Bonaparte, fooled for a time, as he himself admitted, was placed in a quandary. Could he reinforce Vaubois without courting disaster at Verona, and *vice versa?* He was not strong enough to dominate both sectors at the same time.

Deciding that Alvintzi was the greater peril in view of the size of his army and his proximity to Mantua (he had defeated the defenders of Verona at Caldiero on 11 November), Bonaparte reconcentrated his troops to fight the battle of Arcola on 15-17 November.

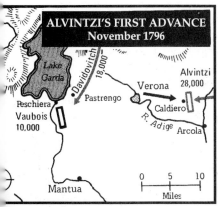

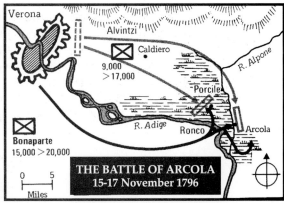

The Battle of Rivoli, 14 January 1797 - a romanticised reconstruction; in the background is the Osteria Gorge, scene of the key engagement.

This famous engagement was Napoleon's severest test to date. Throughout its three-day course, Bonaparte had to take careful note of what was taking place on the distant Vaubois sector, and be ready to disengage and rush northwards at short notice to avert disaster. This alone ruled out any scheme of bold manoeuvre on a large scale against Alvintzi, currently at the gateways of Verona, and made Arcola basically an attritional operation. The situation was also complicated by the fact that he could spare barely nine thousand men to contain Würmser's twenty-three thousand within Mantua. He was caught between three fires with a vengeance.

First, on the night of 14 November, Bonaparte marched his men south and east from Verona along the south bank of the Adige, to force a surprise crossing at Ronco - as if to threaten Alvintzi's communications - in the early hours of the 15th. After crossing the

The struggle for the bridge at Arcola, November 1796. Bonaparte seizes a tricolor to rally his tiring men for a new effort.

river, Bonaparte sent Massena's division north-west to secure his flank near Porcile, and himself accompanied Augereau through the marshes in what proved to be a day-long attempt to seize the bridge at Arcola. The French had just gained local ascendancy over the Austrians in both sectors, when Bonaparte felt bound to withdraw them, at dusk, over the Adige, ready to march to Vaubois's aid if necessary. As no ill-tidings had arrived from the north as yet, the second day saw the French fighting to regain the ground voluntarily given up the previous evening. By this time, Alvintzi was in full retreat from Verona. A French attempt to find a river crossing to the south, so as to turn the Austrian left flank, failed, and in the evening Bonaparte again ordered a withdrawal to the south bank. Both sides had now sustained heavy casualties.

Early on the 17th, Bonaparte ordered up part of the thin force besieging Würmser in Mantua to find a crossing well to the south. When the battle reopened, he sent only a small force to hold the Porcile flank, and massed the greater part of two divisions in an ambush position along the dykes facing Arcola. The Austrians, surprised, were driven from the bridge at last; Bonaparte - in the

André Massena (1752-1817), who later became a marshal, and was created Duc de Rivoli and Prince Essling. He was one of Napoleon's ablest subordinates.

thick of the fighting - was almost flung into the dyke, but was rescued by his aides. Meanwhile, Augereau had found a ford near the confluence of the Adige and Alpone, and a tough afternoon battle developed against Alvintzi's main body, which had been diverted south to join the fighting. The day was won by the French when a small party of cavalry made a noisy appearance from the east, simulating a larger force, and the simultaneous approach of French troops from the Mantua garrison in the south induced Alvintzi to order a precipitate retreat towards Vicenza. Over the three days' fighting, the French had lost some 4,500 men, the Austrians 7,000.

This boldly-handled battle had averted a crisis near Verona and, at last, Napoleon was able to rush troops to Vaubois's aid. The Austrian troops threatening Vaubois were repulsed on 21 November; stability again returned; and the siege of Mantua continued unabated.

But the Austrians remained determined to retain Mantua. Würmser, within the city, was already experiencing disease amid the unhealthy marshes - reasons which explain his largely passive role during the excitements of November - but he would still entertain no thought of capitulation. Alvintzi, licking his wounds near Bassano, was soon at work rebuilding an army of forty-five thousand men ready for yet another campaign. As for the French, following the failure of Moreau's and Jourdan's offensives, the Directory was increasingly desirous of patching up peace, and north Italy remained the only highly active front: it had become, in fact, the major sector of the war. Some reinforcements reached Bonaparte during December, building his strength to perhaps fifty-five thousand men, but of these ten thousand were permanently assigned to the siege of Mantua, and as many more were needed to garrison an increasingly restive Milanese and keep open vital lines of communication.

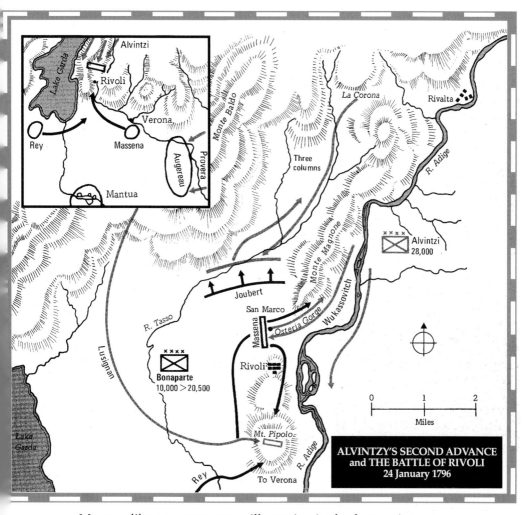

Mantua, like a magnet, was still exerting its fatal attraction upon
the Austrian War Council, and in early January 1797 Alvintzi was
once more on the march through the Alpine passes, this time in no
less than five columns, not counting a diversion of nine thousand
men approaching from the east under General Provera. Soon
Augereau, from Legnano, and Joubert, near La Corona, were
reporting major enemy pressure on their sectors. Still Bonaparte
held his hand, waiting for the situation to clarify itself: he could not
afford to misconstrue the main Austrian line of attack.

The French reserve - Massena's and Rey's divisions - thus waited
near Verona. Would they be ordered north to Lake Garda or east
towards Legnano? On 13 January Bonaparte realised that the north
was the vital sector. 'The enemy's plan is at last unmasked - he is
marching with considerable forces on Rivoli.' All but three

Etching of the wily Talleyrand, ex-Bishop of Autun. An unscrupulous politician always fully concerned with his own survival, he was nevertheless an able foreign minister.

thousand men, left to garrison Verona, hurried north to reinforce Joubert's hard-pressed holding force.

The battlefield of Rivoli lies on a steep plateau to the west of the Adige, linked to the river by the steep Osteria Gorge. As Alvintzi's five columns, jointly some twenty-eight thousand men strong, converged on the area, Bonaparte rushed ahead of his hastening columns to join Joubert's ten thousand men by 2 am on the 14th. By 8 am this force had been boosted to seventeen thousand and eighteen guns by the arrival of Massena, and Bonaparte at once precipitated the battle by launching Joubert and part of Massena's men in a wasting attack against the first three Austrian columns, some twelve thousand strong, as they began to breast the Trombalore Heights on the northern edge of the plateau. After a stiff fight, these columns were checked. Meanwhile one of Joubert's brigades had occupied the head of the Osteria Gorge, while the remainder of Massena's division was held in reserve around Rivoli, with orders to watch the Tasso valley to the immediate west of the plateau.

Simultaneously, the remaining three Austrian columns appeared from different directions. The easternmost column mounted guns east of the Adige; another, under Wukassovitch, began to storm up the Osteria Gorge; and the third, under Lusignan, suddenly appeared from the south below Rivoli. Desperate fighting ensued, with the French under attack from three quarters, but on no single sector were the dispersed Austrians strong enough to achieve lasting success. The main crisis centred around the village of San Marco, where seven thousand Austrians were making headway against the tiring French. Suddenly an Austrian ammunition waggon exploded in the midst of their column. Seizing the opportunity afforded by the stunned reaction, the French mounted a determined charge by five hundred infantry and cavalry; ten minutes later the gorge was cleared.

It only remained to deal with Lusignan's attack. By midday his four thousand men had been neatly trapped between Massena's troops and the newly-arrived three-thousand-strong advance guard of Rey, coming up from Lake Garda. Three thousand Austrians were taken prisoner.

By 5 pm the battle was won. The Austrians, losing in all fourteen thousand men, were in full retreat for the north, pursued throughout the following day by Joubert. The French, who had lost perhaps five thousand men, pressed on. As Vaubois pushed north, Bonaparte hastened south, intent on intercepting the secondary Austrian force as it forced Augereau back to the approaches to Mantua. During the period of the 13th to 16th, Massena's division covered fifty-four miles of ground and fought in three engagements. Provera was caught on the very threshold of Mantua at La Favorita late on the 15th. Würmser's sortie the next day proved abortive, and Provera surrendered with six thousand men.

It was the end, at last, for Mantua. On 2 February Würmser and sixteen thousand men formally surrendered, and a further fourteen thousand were too sick to march out. North Italy, after ten months' fighting, was now almost all within French control.

Yet Vienna still refused to come to terms with the French Republic and sent Archduke Charles, almost as youthful a commander as Bonaparte himself, to form a new army in the Frioul. The Directory had by now reversed their idea of strategic priorities, and afforded the Army of Italy precedence over the German front, and soon Bonaparte had some sixty thousand men to face fifty thousand Austrians. Without Mantua to contend with, all his efforts could be devoted to the final stage of the campaign. Using Joubert to threaten repeated envelopments with twenty thousand men operating eastwards and into the Tyrol from Trent, Bonaparte drove the Archduke back from the River Tagliamento on 16 March, and then proceeded to press him back from river-line to river-line, as the French swept devastatingly through the eastern Alps. Eventually, Charles took the dangerous decision to divide his army; as a result, part fell into Massena's hands in the Pass of Tarvis, while the rest were pressed back towards Leoben. By this stage, Bonaparte's impetus was wholly exhausted, and there was still no news of Moreau's delayed German offensive, and so the French halted on 7 April at the Semmering Pass, only seventy-five miles from Vienna. Bonaparte turned to diplomacy, and reached agreement for a five-day armistice, extended on the 13th for a further five. On 17 April, the Austrian government agreed to sign the Preliminaries of Leoben, and in October the formal Peace of

Frustration in the Orient

Napoleon was always fascinated by the Orient, scene of the achievements of Alexander the Great and many another ancient hero. At one time he even planned to serve the Turkish Sultan. In 1798, however, his chance to visit the Levant materialised. Hoping to threaten British possessions in India, the Directory authorised him to attack and occupy Egypt. The expedition brought him great achievements and even greater predicaments.

After conquering Egypt, he invaded Syria. His army contracted bubonic plague, and in an heroic gesture Bonaparte insisted on visiting his sick soldiers in the Pestiferies of Jaffa. Eventually he was forced to retreat back into Egypt.

Two British sailors contributed to the overall failure of Bonaparte in the Orient. Horatio Nelson (left) after missing the French transports at sea, fought and destroyed their battle-fleet at the Nile, 2 August 1798, effectively cutting the expedition off from France. Commodore Sir William Sydney Smith RN (right) later captured the French siege-guns and reinforced the defenders of Acre. The two sailors, however, distasted each other.

Smith also kept Bonaparte informed of the disasters befalling France in Europe. On 22 August 1799, he left for France. Cruikshank's cartoon depicts Bonaparte slinking away from Egypt, deserting his unsuspecting army.

The French expedition included many scientists and other experts. An important discovery was the Rosetta Stone which was later captured by the British. This provided the key to the hieroglyphics of Ancient Egypt.

Campo Formio was signed. By this the Austrians ceded control of Belgium, the western Rhine enclaves, the Ionian Isles, and in Italy, Milan, Bologna and Modena, which were formed into the new Cisalpine Republic under French domination. France returned Istria, Dalmatia and the Frioul, and evacuated the Republic of Venice, thus leaving Austria a foothold in Italy - practically a guarantee of future conflict.

General Bonaparte had now established his reputation as France's most gallant soldier. His stupendous military career was well underway. His military ideas had been tried out and tested, and adapted in the light of experience. Almost every aspect of war had been involved in this year-long campaign, and at its close it can be claimed that Bonaparte's apprenticeship was over. The Eagle had found wings, beak and talons.

After several months spent in reordering the affairs of the new Cisalpine Republic, the successful general returned to receive the plaudits of Paris. Lionised by society, and mockingly nicknamed 'Puss-in-Boots' by the coquettes on account of his lean and somewhat gangling appearance, large hat and even larger footwear, the honour which particularly pleased Bonaparte was his election to membership of France's most scholarly body, the Institute. Typically, however, an inactive life was not to his liking, and he was pleased to accept command of the army drawn up along the Channel coast ready to invade Great Britain. Now that Austria had left the Coalition (Spain and Prussia had made separate peaces in 1795), the British were the last foe left in the lists. However, a rapid tour of the Channel ports convinced Bonaparte that the Royal Navy's supremacy made a serious crossing out of the question.

The Directory had no option but to accept the verdict. It could not risk a fiasco, but it was equally aware of the need to 'make war pay

The battle of the Pyramids, 1798, by General Lejeune. Note the six-deep divisional squares in action. This tactical formation was devised by Bonaparte to meet the massed charges of the Mameluke horsemen in Egypt. This decisive victory won Cairo for the French.

for war', and certainly did not wish to have a young firebrand, already a legend to his men, finding time to enter the academic political intrigues, with an idle army standing waiting behind him. It was at the suggestion of the sage and experienced politician Talleyrand that an ancient scheme for attacking England indirectly through an invasion of Egypt - thus destroying the British Levant trade by pressure upon the inefficient Turkish regime and even possibly mounting a threat towards India - was eagerly adopted. Nobody was more excited by this plan than Bonaparte, who had always been fascinated by the East; and under great secrecy an expedition of some thirty-six thousand men was soon massing at Toulon, Genoa and Civita Vecchia, together with over three hundred savants (scholars, civilian engineers, scientists - even a poet and a composer were in the party), carefully selected. Years later, Bonaparte described his inspiration as follows:

> *In Egypt I found myself freed from the obstacles of an irksome civilisation. I was full of dreams. I saw myself founding a religion, marching into Asia, riding an elephant a turban on my head and in my hand a new Koran that I would have composed to suit my need. The time I spent in Egypt was the most beautiful of my life because it was the most ideal.*

This highly-romantic conception - or even misrepresentation - was

The battle of Aboukir, 25 July 1798, a short, sharp battle near Alexandria against the Turks, who were swept back and driven into the Mediterranean.

A French storming-party being repulsed from the breach at Acre, 'the key to Palestine'. British sailors took an active part in the defence.

not going to be shared by most of those who accompanied him on his quest, but there is no question that scholarly and civilising motives as well as military ambitions lay beneath his determination to visit the Orient.

To protect the operation, a cover plan was devised, indicating Ireland as the possible objective. The troops massed at the designated embarkation points and naval vessels prepared to escort the forming convoys. On 19 May 1798, the ships put to sea, an off-

shore gale most conveniently driving away the watchful frigates of Rear-Admiral Nelson. Thus the expedition's fear of being intercepted by the Royal Navy's Mediterranean squadron was allayed. The convoys made their way to the various *rendezvous,* and on 9 June the combined fleet gathered off the island of Malta, where the token resistance of the Knights of St John was quickly quelled; and, leaving a French garrison behind, the fleet sailed on.

Nelson, by this time, was scouring the seas for the enemy, but his very speed acted to slow the convoy's advantage. The paths of the two fleets crossed late on the 22nd and again on 27 June - but fate remained almost miraculously kind to the French. While Nelson toured the coastline of Anatolia, the French sailed south-east for Alexandria, and between 1 and 3 July the transports unloaded their relieved human cargoes near Marabout. Little opposition was initially encountered from the Mamelukes - the *de facto* rulers of Egypt - but Alexandria had to be fought for on 2 July. Bonaparte did not linger there long. Sending Desaix to seize Rosetta in the Delta, and thereafter to operate up the Nile, Bonaparte led the remainder of the army in a desperate and thirsty seventy-two hour march over the desert towards Damanhur. The near-mutinous force reached the Nile near Rahmaniya on the 10th, where Desaix's force also arrived on the 12th. Next day there was a sharp skirmish with four thousand Mamelukes under Murad Bey at Shubra Khit, and with a Moslem flotilla on the Nile, but the French were victorious. Cairo was now Bonaparte's objective and by 20 July he was within a day's march of the city. Facing him, near the pyramids, stood massed the forces of the Beys, perhaps a hundred thousand in all, although only eighteen thousand, including six thousand Mamelukes, were drawn up on the west bank of the Nile immediately in the French path.

The battle of the Pyramids, fought the next day, resulted in a decisive victory. The feudal Mamelukes stood no chance before the disciplined fire of the French divisional squares, drawn up in a new formation devised by their commanding general himself. For 390 casualties, the French inflicted some five thousand. The French occupied Cairo, while Murad Bey and his three thousand surviving Mameluke cavalry fled for Middle Egypt.

Sending Desaix on what was to prove a heroic expedition to conquer Upper Egypt, Bonaparte set himself and his civilian experts to work refashioning Egyptian life and institutions. The work was interrupted, however, by the arrival of grave news from the coast: on 2 August Nelson's battlefleet had engaged and largely destroyed Bruey's squadrons at the battle of the Nile. This meant that the French army was now isolated from France, and the news sent a shudder of apprehension through the homesick troops. Work was resumed, only to be even more rudely interrupted on 21 October, when the people of Cairo rose in revolt. Its suppression cost the French three hundred lives, and a brutal retribution was exacted. Outbreaks of bubonic plague added further to French misery.

But Bonaparte was soon beset by even graver problems. Encouraged by the Nile, the Sultan of Turkey had declared a Holy War against the French infidel, and soon news was reaching Cairo of two Turkish armies preparing to invade Egypt. One, under the Pasha of Damascus, was gathering in Syria. The other was massing in Rhodes. It was never Napoleon's way to wait upon events. Deeming the Army of Damascus to represent the graver peril, he determined to attack it outside Egypt before the Army of Rhodes could intervene. Leaving Desaix and a total of perhaps twenty thousand men to occupy Egypt, on 6 February 1799, Bonaparte led four weak divisions from Katia into the Sinai Desert. The need to take El Arish caused an eleven-day delay, but by the 23rd the expedition was in Syria. Gaza was occupied two days later, and Jaffa fell to a storm on 7 March. This success was sullied by the cold-blooded massacre of almost five thousand prisoners, who Bonaparte claimed had broken parole granted in earlier operations.

Plague now struck the French with full force, and Bonaparte visited the hospitals, at great personal risk, to restore morale. Leaving their sick behind them, the army marched on for Haifa on 14 March, its next objective being the port and fortress of Acre. Here they found themselves faced by a determined defence by Djezzar Pasha, in fact inspired by a British naval officer, Commodore Sir William Sydney Smith, whose two ships-of-war added their crews and guns to strengthen the town's defences. After a number of assaults had been driven back, Bonaparte was compelled to have recourse to regular siege methods, but this too was hampered by the Royal Navy which intercepted and captured half the French heavy artillery, being brought up by sea. The cannon were then used to strengthen the defences.

As the siege dragged on, the number of plague cases grew. Then news arrived that the Army of Damascus was approaching. This constituted a challenge more to Napoleon's liking, and to avert the danger of being ground between the upper and the nether mill-stones, he sent out strong detachments to reconnoitre. One of these, led by General Kléber, ran into the main Turkish army, perhaps thirty-five thousand strong, near Mount Tabor. Kléber's fifteen hundred men gamely engaged the mighty host, and afforded Bonaparte enough time to bring up Bon's division from Acre, twenty-five miles away. The resultant battle on 16 April saw 4,500 Frenchmen inflict some seven thousand casualties and rout the foe for the loss of less than a hundred men. Thus the strategic purpose of the invasion of Syria had been achieved; one threat to a French-controlled Egypt had been driven back.

Acre remained as intractable a problem as ever, and on 20 May Bonaparte decided to cut his losses and abandon the siege. A traumatic withdrawal towards Egypt began, but at last on 3 June the half-starved survivors limped back into Katia. By the 14th the battered little army, perhaps one-third smaller than when it had set out, was back in Cairo. Soon revolts against French rule were springing up everywhere, but these were put down with accustomed ferocity. Then, in mid-July, news arrived from the coast that the Army of Rhodes had at last landed near Alexandria. Bonaparte rushed to the coast with all available men, and on 25 July routed the new foe at the hard-fought battle of Aboukir. The survivors re-embarked and sailed away, but this success had cost the French some 970 killed and wounded - losses which the rapidly-dwindling army could ill afford.

Bonaparte was now increasingly aware of, and worried by, his isolation. The news from France was very bad, and Commodore Smith deliberately had old newspapers sent ashore to his rival from which he learned of a rapidly-worsening situation. It was no time for a man of ambition to be away from the central arena at which, in a climate of uncertainty, careers would be made or broken with every shifting wind. He determined not be be overtaken by events and, in the greatest secrecy, laid his plans to slip away from Egypt and return to France. And so, on 22 August, he set sail, accompanied by a handful of confidants and staff officers, leaving the disconsolate Army of Egypt to the command of an enraged Kléber. For propaganda purposes, Napoleon declared that he had gone to seek reinforcements and a new fleet, but few were fooled for long.

CHAPTER THREE

The Years of Achievement
1800-07

Napoleon's journey home lasted six weeks, until on 9 October, he landed at Fréjus and at once headed for Paris. There his first crisis was not a public but a private affair, for Josephine had made little secret of her infidelities during his absence. A painful scene developed, and at one point the jealous husband wanted to end the marriage in divorce. But in the end he relented, won over by Josephine's pleas and entreaties. He himself had not been blameless, and in Egypt had found consolation with Madame Fourés, the wife of one of his lieutenants. And so the marriage was saved, though from this point it became one of detached tolerance on both sides, one of mutual convenience, and a long way from the frenzied passion which had first inspired the young suitor.

Meanwhile, the Directory greeted Napoleon's unexpected return with reserve. Some spoke of charging him with desertion, though his popularity was such that no one spoke very loudly. It was a

The three Consuls-Cambacères, Bonaparte and Lebrun, 1800. Bonaparte was soon the only one that mattered.

critical time for the government. Administrative incompetence and financial weakness combined to undermine its authority. Moreover, a new war, that of the Second Coalition, had broken out in the course of 1799. Encouraged by the battle of the Nile, Great Britain had pursuaded, and linked, other powers to join her against the French, and now Russian and Austrian armies were in the field against her.

The result was a political *coup* against the regime which, for the first time, brought Napoleon to political power. One of the Directors, the ageing, subtle Siéyès, laid the plan. He chose Napoleon, and the General agreed, to be his 'sword'. It was a confusing affair, in which Napoleon himself played a muddled and undistinguished part. At one point, he narrowly escaped death when he descended on the Council of Five Hundred, one of the main constitutional assemblies. He was saved only by the timely intervention of his soldiers and by the presence of mind of the Council's President, his own brother Lucien. Yet, by the evening of 9 November, 18 Brumaire by the Revolutionary Calendar, the coup had been accomplished. A new constitution was created, dominated by three Consuls, Siéyès, another former Director, Roger-Ducos and Napoleon himself.

The First Consul, portrait by Gros. One of the few portraits for which Napoleon sat.

It was a victory for authority against the Jacobin element; and there quickly followed a second victory: that of Napoleon over his new colleagues, for if the inspiration had belonged to Siéyès, the power belonged to the armed forces and their leader. There could be no opposition when Napoleon, urged on by his own growing belief in his destiny, manoeuvred his fellow-Consuls into retirement within a few short months. Two nonentities replaced them, and the Constitution was once again re-written to place all real authority in the hands of the First Consul, Napoleon. In February 1800 a national plebiscite voted on this new Constitution. Three million were in favour, fifteen hundred dissented. France had given herself a dictatorship in all but name.

A period of frantic activity now began. Rewards were showered on the faithful; the opposition was either won over or made to disappear. The First Consul also launched forth on a series of major reforms which began the remodelling of French life. But the cunning Corsican knew that he could set the seal upon his exalted position only by giving the French people what they craved most - namely peace through victory in the field. This he set out to obtain, and under cover of peace negotiations he began to prepare a new campaign against Austria. Moreau would attack on the Upper Rhine; a new army, called the Reserve, began to collect around Dijon under the normal command of General Berthier. Its intended destination would be Italy; its real commander Bonaparte himself.

Napoleon was helped when Prussia, who had in any case failed to field an army, backed out of the coalition, and by Russian agreements with Vienna, which effectively left only Austria to deal with on the Continent itself. Austria had two main armies in the field: 120,000 men under General Kray in Germany, and some ninety-seven thousand under General Melas in north Italy. They planned to use the former in a defensive role while the latter exploited Italian discontent with French rule, consolidated earlier gains, marched on Genoa and ultimately threatened Toulon.

Any such possibilities Bonaparte was determined to avert. He intended to launch a rapid attack to snatch a quick victory, making the fullest use of the advantages offered by French-dominated Switzerland, its passes and rivers, to move a force into the rear of one or other of the major Austrian field armies. Moreau, commanding some 120,000 men on the Rhine, was not eager to have the First Consul operating on his sector, and obstructed plans for the Army of the Reserve, some fifty thousand strong, to be

employed in this direction. Meanwhile, in north Italy, General Massena and the forty thousand men of the Army of Liguria, suddenly found themselves under heavy pressure as Melas launched his offensive, on 5 April, and soon were sundered in two, half being driven back beyond the Var, the rest tightly besieged in Genoa.

With commendable flexibility, the First Consul adjusted to circumstances. The Reserve would now sweep south over the Alps,

Napoleon crossing the Alps on mule back - the reality, as painted by Delaroche.

reinforced by a single corps from the Rhine, to force a decisive battle on Melas. While Massena in Genoa attracted his attention, the Reserve would appear over the Alps to cut Melas's links with Mantua and Austria, and fall upon his rear. By early May, as the siege became ever more desperate for the defenders, the Reserve was moved into Switzerland ready for its bold advance. Executive orders had been issued to both Moreau and Berthier on 24 April; next day the former at last crossed the Rhine, and by 13 May the Austrians were in full retreat eastwards, abandoning their links with Melas.

This was the moment which Bonaparte had been waiting for. Without pausing for General Lecourbe's dilatory corps to join him from Germany, he ordered his army into the Alpine passes in five columns on the 14th. Although such manoeuvres had happened

The artist David portrayed a heroic Napoleon crossing the Alps. The element of propaganda is important in this version.

several times in previous campaigns, this passage was unusually early in the year, and special measures had to be taken to pass the guns through the ice and snow at the head of the Great St Bernard Pass - the route used by the main column. The summit was safely passed, the First Consul crossing over on mule-back on the 15th, and the next day his advance guard was through Aosta, driving before it several Austrian detachments. But on 10 May a snag developed, when the French encountered a determined garrison in Fort Bard, blocking the only practicable road. For five days the main impetus of the French advance was checked, and all attacks failed; but on 25 and 26 May six cannon were spirited past the fort at dead of night, to join the infantry divisions which had already avoided the obstacle by mountain routes, and Bonaparte pressed ahead to Ivrea, leaving a force to blockade Fort Bard, which managed to hold out until 5 June.

The immediate French objective was now to capture munitions

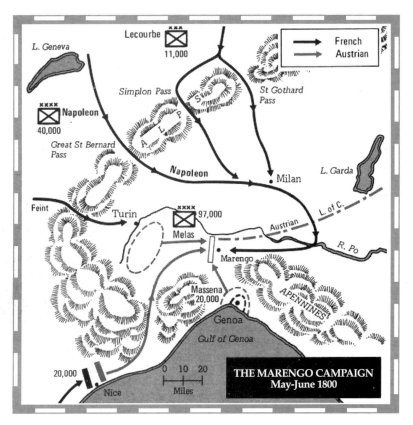

and cannon to replace those bottled up beyond Bard, so instead of marching directly on Genoa they headed for Milan. The city was occupied on 2 June, and it was now that Lecourbe at last appeared with eleven thousand men to swell the French forces. Bonaparte also transferred his communications to the safer St Gotthard Pass. The Reserve then moved towards the River Po, crossing near Piacenza between 7 and 9 June, before swinging west towards the strategic objective of Stradella - possession of which would place them straight across Melas's communications.

Melas, meanwhile, had been on the point of calling off the siege of Genoa to guard his rear when Massena, despairing of relief, surrendered on 4 June. The news reached the First Consul on 7 June in captured despatches. He was deeply disturbed - for his enemy could now use Genoa as a refuge - and might even be evacuated by sea with the aid of the Royal Navy - and either event would rob the French of the decisive success they were seeking. Bonaparte's

The battle of Marengo, 14 June 1800. General Desaix is struck from his horse (left background) at the moment of victory. The artist, the future General Lejeune, has included himself mounted with the white brassard, (foreground right). His paintings are among the best for the Napoleonic period.

solution was to press ahead past Stradella towards the town of Alessandria, where a large part of the Austrian army was reported to be concentrating. On the way, a brisk action was fought against the Austrian Ott at Montebello on 8 June, but by the 13th the French had crossed the River Scrivia, and had also been joined - at last - by most of their guns from Ivrea. The French pressed on towards Marengo through heavy rain.

Still fearing that Melas might attempt to escape either to the north bank of the Po or alternatively make a break south towards Genoa, and never for a moment anticipating an attack, the First Consul detached Lapoype's division from the Reserve, to seize the Po crossings on the 13th, and in the early hours of the 14th similarly sent off Desaix with another division to move south on Novi and block the road to Genoa. These decisions reduced the Reserve's front-line strength to barely 24,100 men and fifteen guns - and almost led to a major catastrophe for the French that day. For, far from seeking to escape, General Melas decided to attack, and issued out of Marengo, thirty-one thousand strong, over concealed pontoon bridges which had escaped the notice of French patrols the previous evening. By 7 am, the battle had begun.

Napoleon at first thought that the Austrian advance was a feint designed to cover a withdrawal. By nine o'clock, however, he had realised his error, and urgent orders of recall were sent off to Lapoype and Desaix. 'I had thought to attack Melas', ran the cryptic message to Desaix. 'He has attacked me first. For God's sake come up if you still can.' The tone gives some measure of the urgency of the hour. By midday, the outnumbered and fast tiring divisions of Lannes and Victor were being forced to give ground from Marengo and fall back eastwards towards San Giuliano. There were also threatening indications that a column commanded by General Ott, 7,500 strong, was intending to work its way round the French northern flank.

After a brief lull, the outflanking danger had become a reality, and Bonaparte was forced to send his last reserves - the troops of General Monnier and the Consular Guard - to extend his right wing in an attempt to meet the menace, near Castel Ceriolo. This earned a brief respite, but on the far left Victor's troops, now running short of ammunition, were being pressed back remorselessly and the French line continued to reel back in growing disarray. The First Consul was tireless in his efforts to rally his men, but by 2.30 pm it seemed as if all his efforts would be to no avail as the Austrian centre and right, smelling victory, paused to re-form into a huge column, ready to crash through the weary French.

But help was at hand. A little before three o'clock, a mud-spattered General Desaix rode up ahead of his men, to announce their impending arrival. Fortunately for the French, Desaix's progress towards Novi had been delayed by a flooded river and it seems that he was already 'marching for the sound of the cannon' when the urgent message of recall found him. (Lapoype, by contrast, received his message only at 6 pm.) 'This battle is completely lost', commented the newcomer cryptically, 'but it is only two [in fact it was three] o'clock; there is time to win another.'

At length, by 5pm, General Boudet's division of 5,300 foot-sore but battle-fresh men, together with their eight guns, had arrived near San Giuliano from the south, and were drawn up behind the exhausted Victor. At this juncture, the aged Melas decided to hand over command of the Austrian army to his second-in-command, General Zach, and retired to Alessandria. Then, in leisurely and complacent fashion, the massive Austrian column began to advance. To meet it came Desaix at the head of his men, drawn up in *l'ordre mixte* by demi-brigades, left flank forward. At this precise moment a French shot caused several Austrian ammunition waggons to explode. As had happened at a similar critical moment at Rivoli, the Austrians hesitated. The French snatched at the fleeting opportunity; Marmont rushed up eight guns to the front, and opened close-range fire at the reeling column. Kellerman wheeled four hundred cavalry into line, and with a loud cheer plunged into the flank of the Austrian column, while Desaix and his infantry came rushing forward, bayonets levelled. Just before the lines met, Desaix fell, mortally wounded, but the impact of his attack was irresistible, and the whole French line, heartened by this change of fortune, swept forward with a cheer. This abrupt reversal of the tide of battle was too much for the Austrians, and by 6 pm they were in full flight for the safety of Alessandria and its hundred guns. For a loss of seven thousand casualties, the French remained the victorious possessors of the field, having inflicted fourteen thousand casualties (including eight thousand prisoners) and captured forty guns. Next day, Melas sued for an armistice, and in return for leave to retire to the east of the River Ticino abandoned Genoa and the Milanese.

'Marengo was a lesson', Bonaparte once admitted in an honest moment. Defeat had been very near, and but for Desaix's timely arrival the outcome would have been grim. Over the years, Napoleon was continually taking pains to represent Marengo as a major success, its various phases being deliberately planned in advance. In successive rewritings of the official account, he fabricated the idea of a deliberate withdrawal by the French left, designed to draw the Austrians towards an approaching Desaix, who was carefully placed so as to outflank them at the moment at which they were farthest from their bridges. Such was the gist of his account in 1803. Two years later, Napoleon was prepared to claim that the French right had never lost control of Castel Ceriolo, but had used it as the anchor for the controlled swing of the French line towards San Giuliano, at the same time setting up a new line of communications, or of retreat, towards the River Po and General Lapoype. These developments in the story were almost wholly bogus, but the ideas upon which they were based would, as we shall see, be built into the *Grande Armée's* devastating system of Grand Tactics. The outcome of 14 June 1800, however, was owing almost wholly to the First Consul's subordinate commanders, and most especially the loyal Desaix, rather than to his own efforts. Nevertheless, he could still learn from his errors, though he already

*'The plumb-pudding in danger' - famous cartoon by Gillray. William Pitt
helps himself to the oceans (symbolising British naval supremacy) while
Napoleon serves himself Europe with the aid of his sabre.*

found them hard to admit. Thus Marengo became part of the
legend.

Marengo regained much of north Italy for the French, but it did
not win the war. Three more campaigns had to be launched by
Generals Moreau, Brune and Macdonald before victory was
assured. The First Consul had meantime returned to Paris (by a
constitutional rule he had technically been barred from taking
command in the field as First Consul, and throughout the campaign
to date had posed as Berthier's adviser). The struggle dragged on as
inconclusive peace negotiations continued at Leoben. But French
pressure proved remorseless, culminating in Moreau's victory at
Hohenlinden on 3 December, and Murat's drive into Tuscany and
the Papal States. On 8 February 1801, hostilities at length came to an
end in the Peace of Luneville, which effectively restored the
situation of Campo Formio; although the French added the duchy
of Parma to the Cisalpine Republic, compensating the Duke with
Tuscany. Further territorial adjustments were made along the
Rhine, but in many ways it was a moderate peace.

Once again, a Coalition had collapsed about the ears of England's
premier, William Pitt, who was forced to resign in March 1801. Since

the beginning of that month, however, a British expeditionary force had been landed in Egypt, and by September Bonaparte's former comrades had been driven to accept a negotiated capitulation, by which they were to be allowed repatriation. The First Consul, meanwhile, had been negotiating for some months with British representatives at Amiens, and before the final news from Egypt had broken, the Preliminaries of Amiens had been signed on 1 October 1801. A formal Peace Treaty followed in February 1802, and the First Consul could claim that he had honoured his promise to bring peace through victory. For a brief spell, Europe was not at war, and a grateful French people voted on 2 August 1802, to appoint Bonaparte, the 'Peace-Maker', Consul for life. A crown and throne now lay only one step away.

Some time before the signature of peace with Great Britain, Bonaparte had launched forth on that great series of reforms, legal, economic, social and constitutional, which together constitute his most constructive and most lasting work. As great a statesman as he was a solder, he daringly carried through a Concordat with the Pope in 1801 whereby France returned to the Catholic fold, and the following year saw the emergence of the great Codes which refashioned almost every aspect of French life and many parts of which remain the basis of French Civil Law to the present day. Commissions of experts examined and enquired, their deliberations often chaired by the head of state in person, whose grasp of many complex and specialist subjects and issues often astounded his advisers.

Sensing a need for some system of rewarding the deserving, Bonaparte instituted the *Légion d'Honneur* in 1801, creating military and civil branches. 'It is with baubles that men are led', he declared. Rewards were showered on the loyal and able generals, culminating in the establishment of the Marshalate in 1804; the same year saw the first steps towards the creation of a new nobility. At the same time, remaining centres of opposition, whether die-hard republican or convinced royalist were steadily eliminated by the secret police apparatus wielded by Fouché. Censorship of the Press, spying and 'tuning the pulpit' remained in force. On the other hand, such unpopular instruments as the infamous Law of Suspects were repealed, and *émigrés* who would return to serve the new regime were restored to at least part of their estates.

Of course, the Consul became the target of much bitter criticism - and several assassination attempts by both Royalists and left-wing Jacobins. He escaped a bomb explosion on his way to the Opera in

'It is with baubles that men are led.' Napoleon awards the first decorations of the Légion d' Honneur at a ceremony at the Invalides Palace, 15 July 1803.

December 1800, and 1803 saw the exposure of the notorious Cadoudal conspiracy which had been planned with British connivance. These incidents were used by his propagandists to prepare the way for the suspension of the Constitution and the replacement of the Consulate by the Empire. Already Consul for life, Napoleon now took the next logical step, nominally to safeguard the regime, by founding a new dynasty. And so the proposal to make Napoleon Emperor was put to the test in a national plebiscite in 1804. The outcome was never in doubt, and on 18 May he was duly proclaimed Emperor. The coronation was performed on 2 December 1804, but although the Pope was brought to Paris for the ceremony, Napoleon insisted on placing the crown on his own head symbolically before crowning Josephine in her turn. This was all a very far cry from the impecunious days of his Corsican childhood. 'If only our father could see us now', Napoleon remarked to Joseph. He was a little over thirty-five years old, and his career had indeed been meteoric.

Yet already France was at war again. Europe's short-lived peace had lasted only until 16 May 1803, when France found herself once more at war with Great Britain over matters of colonial and commercial rivalry. Over the next year, Napoleon massed two hundred thousand men along the Channel coast in the Camp of Boulogne but, as in 1798, his navy could never gain the necessary control of the sea to permit an invasion to be launched. Meanwhile friction steadily grew between France and the Continental powers. The established monarchs would not accept Napoleon's titles or position and absolutely distrusted his further ambitions in Germany where he was building alliances within the southern states, a traditional sphere of Austrian influence. His ruthless methods came to a peak with the execution in 1804 of the Duc d'Enghien, an alleged, though unproven conspirator, who was kidnapped from neutral territory. The general repugnance caused by the crime played its part in helping William Pitt, once again Prime Minister, to form the Third Coalition. British gold persuaded the Francophile Tsar of Russia, Alexander I, to join in April 1805; Sweden agreed to make war on the French, and in June Emperor Francis II of Austria followed suit. It was indeed a coalition of the 'European establishment' against the Emperor, and of the great powers only Prussia remained aloof. Thus Pitt called into being a force of 200,000 Russians and 250,000 Austrians - and in round numbers the Alliance could field half a million men, subsidised by Britain. Following the anticipated Allied victory, France was to be restricted to the frontiers of 1791.

Some conspiracies were real enough. Napoleon narrowly escaped death on his way to the Opera, December 1800, when an 'infernal machine' exploded.

By mid-August 1805, Napoleon had got wind of these developments, and began to transfer troops from the Channel towards the Rhine. He was determined to get his blow in first in central Europe, and rechristened his *'Armée d'Angleterre'*: henceforth, it would be known as *'la Grande Armée'*. Napoleon's intention was to forestall the Allied offensive, and if possible to destroy Austria's armies before the soldiers of the Tsar could arrive in central Europe.

The Austrians were preparing three field armies: ninety-four thousand men were massing in north Italy under the Archduke Charles - Vienna presuming that this theatre would once again see the major French effort; secondly, seventy-two thousand men under Archduke Ferdinand and General Mack were marching on the Danube, intended to eliminate France's ally, Bavaria; a third force, of twenty-two thousand men under the Archduke John, was to be

The Coronation, 2 December 1804. Napoleon insisted on symbolically placing the imperial crown on his own head, and then crowned Josephine. Pope Pius VII was relegated to the role of spectator. Les grandes dames, Napoleon's mother and sisters, look down from the gallery in the rear. 'If only our father could see us now', Napoleon remarked. It was a far cry from the poverty of Corsica.

fielded in the Tyrol, charged with linking the two major war fronts. It was intended that Archduke Charles would initiate the offensive, while Ferdinand and Mack dealt with Bavaria pending the arrival of the Russian forces - first thirty-eight thousand men under General Kutusov, followed by General Buxhowden with forty thousand, with a further twenty thousand under Bennigsen bringing up the rear. Then, massively reinforced, the Austrians would lead their Allies in a major onslaught through the Black Forest to cross the Rhine and move the war into the heartland of France.

Matters were to prove otherwise. Their plans were riddled with false assumptions and shoddy staff work. Napoleon's intention was wholly miscalculated. The Austrians were courting a great risk by moving in Germany and Italy before their Allies had appeared. Moreover the Austrian staff, incredible as it may seem, failed to take into account the ten days' difference between the German and Russian calendars - and their expectation that the Russians would appear by 20 October was to prove a fatal miscalculation.

Meanwhile, Napoleon was massing 210,000 men and 396 guns along and near the Rhine. Subdivided into five *corps d'armée*, the Imperial Guard and the Reserve Cavalry, they quietly took up posts along the west bank stretching from Mainz to Strasbourg; a further corps under Bernadotte was ordered to join the Bavarian forces at Frankfurt and Würzburg, and Augereau was ordered to transfer his VII Corps from Brest as a reserve. The defence of Italy was entrusted to André Massena with some fifty thousand men; he was ordered to hold the Adige line, and keep the Archduke Charles in play. Napoleon's plan for the main army was to execute a massive wheel through Germany towards the Danube once a feint attack into the Black Forest had distracted Ferdinand and Mack. Stuttgart would provide the pivot for the great wheeling movement and the *Grande Armée* would then concentrate along the Danube around Donauwörth before crossing the river to sever the Austrian links with Vienna and force a major battle. Once Mack was destroyed, Napoleon intended to march on Vienna, if necessary fighting the Russians en route, but he was hopeful that their zeal would evaporate once their Austrian allies had been beaten. Massena's role, described as 'the right wing of the *Grande Armée*' was to pin down Charles's larger army, and if possible the Archduke John's as well, until these decisive events had taken place. Such a bold plan called for brilliant staff work and the achievement of a high level of surprise, but Napoleon had every confidence in his army with its

Napoleon's most inveterate opponent was, as ever, Great Britain. From early 1803, a new state of war existed, and Napoleon was soon planning an invasion attempt, forming a vast camp at Boulogne. Below is an engraving of a fanciful project for the invasion, as envisaged by a French artist. Note the use of a Channel tunnel and of a rudimentary form of airborne forces - carried in balloons, using kites for landing. But the picture is accurate in one respect: the line of naval vessels defending Britain's shores was real enough, and failure to secure naval control of the Channel made any project impossible long before Trafalgar was fought. The British authorities took the threat seriously enough however. Right is a broadsheet calling 'undaunted Britons' to prepare to repel the foe, should he land. A popular ballad was composed to heighten morale.

BRITONS TO ARMS !!!

Cheerly my hearts of courage true, the hour's at hand to try your worth: a glorious peril waits for you, and valour pants to lead you forth The battle fleet approaches nigh boys, now some must conquer some must die boys: but that appals not you nor me, for our watch word, it shall be Britons strike home, revenge your country's wrongs, Britons strike home, revenge your country's wrongs.

<table>
<tr><td>

2

Undaunted Britons now shall prove
The Frenchman's folly to invade
Our dearest rights, our country's love,
Our laws, our freedom, and our trade:
On our white cliffs, our colours fly boys,
Which we'll defend, or bravely die boys;
For we are Britons bold and free.
And our watch word it shall be
     Britons strike home &c.

</td><td>

3

The Tyrant Consul then too late
Dismayed shall mourn th' avenging blow,
Let vanquish'd, meet the milder fate
Which mercy grants a fallen foe;
Thus shall the British banners fly boys,
On Albion's cliffs still rais'd on high boys,
And while the gallant flag we see
We'll swear our watch word still shall be
     Britons strike home &c.

</td></tr>
</table>

Published July 30 1803 by John Fairburn N.º 9 Ludgate Street London.

young marshals and eager rank and file; above all, he now controlled a centralised war machine wholly subservient to his will.

By 20 September the French concentration along the Rhine was complete, the same day as the Austrian army, having declared war on Bavaria on the 2nd, occupied the city of Ulm on the Danube. On the 26th, Murat launched his feint attack into the Black Forest region, and, as expected, this served to draw part of the Austrian army to the west. Then, the scene having been successfully set, the main French army crossed the Rhine and set out on its long march through Germany during the night 26-27 September. The web of self-dependent corps, commanded by Bernadotte, Marmont, Davout, Soult, Ney and Lannes, swept on with devastating speed. By 3 October they had occupied a line between Stuttgart and Ansbach, and four days later the leading elements were crossing the Danube at Münster, Donauwörth, Neuburg and Ingolstädt before the startled Austrians realised what was happening. On the 9th, Soult occupied Augsburg, and as the I and III Corps occupied the line of the River Isar as a strategic barrier to block any attempt by the Russians, still well to the east of the Inn, to interfere, Napoleon sent Soult's IV Corps southwards to occupy Memmingen, and thus isolate Ulm from the Archduke John in the Tyrol, while the rest of the army closed in upon Ferdinand and Mack.

The Austrians made a series of rather half-hearted attempts to break out to the north of the Danube, and an error by Murat led to part of Ney's VI Corps finding itself fighting in desperate isolation near Haslach on 11 October, but the superlative fighting by the men of Dupont's division averted catastrophe and the Austrians were repulsed. Napoleon himself was soon at hand to repair the near-breach, and, rebuking Murat, he launched Ney, followed by Lannes's V Corps, in an attack over the key bridge at Elchingen. The Austrian forces were routed on 13 October, and then, remorselessly, the French closed in on the city of Ulm. Meanwhile, Archduke Ferdinand, after a bitter quarrel with Mack, had managed to break out with the Austrian cavalry, but for the remainder there was no escape as the French net closed around the city. Murat's cavalry was soon in hot pursuit of the Archduke, while the French Corps on the northern bank, now reinforced by the arrival of the Imperial Guard in support, took possession of the Michelsberg Heights overlooking the city.

A desperate Mack, still hoping for the arrival of Kutusov from Russia, tried to win time by negotiation, but Napoleon was able to

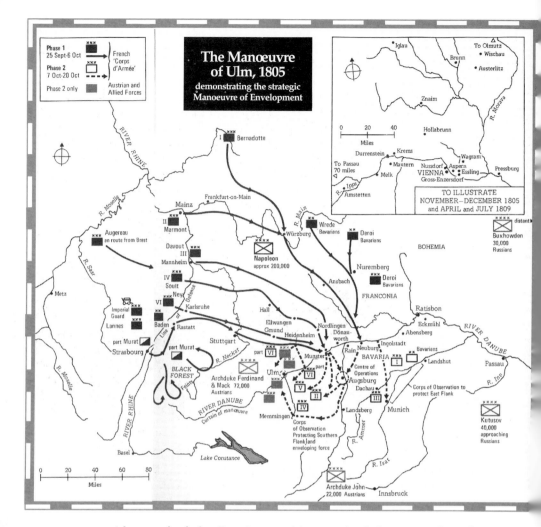

The Manœuvre of Ulm, 1805

demonstrating the strategic Manœuvre of Envelopment

TO ILLUSTRATE
NOVEMBER–DECEMBER 1805
and APRIL and JULY 1809

I Bernadotte

RIVER RHINE

R. Moselle

Augereau en route from Brest

R. Saar

Metz

Frankfurt-on-Main

Mainz

II Marmont

Davout III

Mannheim

IV Soult

Ney VI

Imperial Guard

Lannes

Baden

Rastatt

Karlsruhe

Line of Defence

Stuttgart

part Murat

part Murat

Strasbourg

BLACK FOREST

R. Neckar

Feints

RIVER RHINE

R. Moselle

Basel

Lake Constance

Hall

Ellwangen

Gmund

Heidenheim

Munster

part VI

Ulm

Archduke Ferdinand & Mack 72,000 Austrians

VI

V

II

IV

RIVER DANUBE

Curtain of manœuvre

Memmingen

Corps of Observation Protecting Southern Flank] and enveloping force

R. Ammer

Landsberg

R. Lech

Napoleon approx 200,000

Würzburg

R. Main

Wrede Bavarians

Deroi Bavarians

BOHEMIA

Nuremberg

Ansbach

Deroi Bavarians

FRANCONIA

Nordlingen

Dönauworth

Rain

Neuburg

Ingolstadt

Bavarians

BAVARIA

Centre of Operations

Augsburg

Dachau

III

Munich

Ratisbon

Eckmühl

Abensberg

RIVER DANUBE

I

Landshut

Passau

R. Inn

Corps of Observation to protect East Flank

Iglau

Brunn

Znaim

Hollabrunn

Durrenstein

Krems

To Passau 70 miles

Mautern

Melk

Amstetten

R. Ipps

R. Ens

Wischau

Austerlitz

R. Morava

Wagram

Nussdorf

Aspern

VIENNA

Gross-Enzersdorf

Essling

Pressburg

distant

Buxhowden 30,000 Russians

Archduke John 22,000 Austrians

Innsbruck

R. Isar

Kutusov 40,000 approaching Russians

0   20   40
Miles

0   20   40   60   80
Miles

provide proof of the Russian position, and of the surrender of certain outlying Austrian detachments, and on 17 October Mack agreed to a convention whereby he was to capitulate on the 25th unless help reached him. In fact, Mack was already a beaten and a broken man, and on the 20th, several days ahead of schedule, he surrendered at the head of twenty-seven thousand Austrian troops. Before the month was out, a further thirty thousand (including all Ferdinand's troops) had also been rounded up. In five weeks, Napoleon had eliminated the entire Austrian army without having to fight a major battle. He had mesmerised the enemy by the speed of his movements, the complexity of his strategy and a telling combination of bluff and force. It was virtually a perfect campaign but it still remained to mete out similar treatment to the approaching Russian forces. Furthermore, on 21 October, far away to the west, Admiral Nelson albeit dead had inflicted a massive and famous defeat on Villeneuve's Franco-Spanish fleet off Cape Trafalgar. Napoleon might be well on his way to achieving the mastery of central Germany, but at sea the war was irretrievably lost, and with it any last lingering hopes of mounting an invasion of France's perennial and most determined foe, Great Britain.

But the Emperor was more immediately concerned with the problem of catching Kutusov. That wily warrior, as soon as he learned of Mack's fate, lost no time in retreating, and march as it might, the *Grande Armée* never quite caught up with the Russians. There were a number of rearguard skirmishes at river-lines south of the Danube, but the Tsar's general was always one move ahead. Napoleon was furious to learn that his quarry had successfully withdrawn north of the Danube near Krems by 9 November, while Murat headed for the irrelevant prize of Vienna. Even worse, part of Mortier's newly-created corps was almost trapped at Durrenstein, on the 11th, but managed to fight off almost forty thousand Russians. Another blistering reprimand did not deter Murat from occupying Vienna next day - and by a superb piece of bluff he secured intact the great bridge over the Danube. This windfall assisted the northwards deployment of the Grand Armée, now moving on Hollabrunn, but Kutusov was still determinedly withdrawing towards his *rendezvous* at Znaim with Buxhowden.

The combat at Elchingen, shortly before the surrender of Ulm, October 1805. Marshals Ney and Lannes direct the critical attack on the monastery.

He won more time to achieve this on the 15th after an action near Hollabrunn where General Bagration, commanding the Russian rearguard, fooled Murat with talk of an armistice. Once again, Napoleon was filled with fury at this authorised ceasefire. 'I am lost for words with which to express my displeasure . . . you have thrown away the advantages of the entire campaign.' A chastened Murat at once broke the armistice - only to find that his opponent, after a hard day's fighting at Schöngraben, had eluded him. Even worse, on 20 November Kutusov at last joined up with Buxhowden, making their joint strength some eighty-six thousand men. The chance of defeating the Russians in detail, one by one, had thus eluded the French.

Furthermore, the Emperor's army was now practically exhausted; its battle-strength, after many necessary detachments had been made, was barely fifty-three thousand and Napoleon had to call a halt on the 23rd, after occupying Brünn. He faced an equivocal choice: he could advance no further; to retreat would be to concede defeat; but to hold his ground could prove fatal - as Archdukes Charles and John were now heading for the theatre; and there were strong indications that Prussia was about to declare war on France which would mean a further two hundred thousand troops with whom to contend.

Napoleon, however, was always at his best and most dangerous in a crisis. He at once determined to lure the Russians and Austrians into a precipitate battle near Olmütz, by feigning even greater weakness than was in fact the case. With care he chose a battle position - to the west of the small town of Austerlitz. Then, with consummate skill, he began to lure the Allies towards it, even listening with apparent seriousness to their proposal for a temporary armistice. By the end of November, the Tsar and his hot-headed advisers had fallen for the bait, and the Emperor Francis, also present, had to concur. On 1 December the Allies, 85,400 men and 278 guns strong, marched from Olmütz and occupied the Pratzen Heights, deliberately abandoned by the French. The suspicious Kutusov advocated caution, wanting to wait for the Archdukes; but the Tsar would not contemplate delay.

Napoleon, meanwhile, was developing his own plans. In great secrecy he summoned up Bernadotte's I Corps (thirteen thousand men) from Iglau, and then Davout's III Corps from Vienna. Late on 1 December he had something over seventy-two thousand men in, or near the proposed battle area. He was still fighting at a serious numerical disadvantage, but his situation was far better than the enemy knew. That night, the anniversary of his coronation, Napoleon walked among his ragged troops, receiving a great ovation and an impromptu torchlight procession in his honour.

The French army lay between the main Olmütz-to-Brünn road in the north and the frozen Satschan meres in the south, along a front of almost four miles, with the Goldbach and Bosenitz streams to their front. Most of the men were camped on and behind the Zurlan Height and around the Santon Mound in the north, and only a single division of Soult's IV Corps was in evidence in the southern two miles. This was deliberate, for Napoleon was determined to lure his enemies into a mighty outflanking attack to the south which, if successful, would have severed his links with Vienna. He knew that Davout's approaching corps would reinforce his right wing by early morning, and his whole plan centred upon inducing the bulk of the enemy army to abandon the Pratzen Heights in their centre. Once this was accomplished, he planned to unleash two veteran divisions to seize the centre of the Allied position from which the French would be able to envelop either the enemy right or left wing as circumstances dictated. Meanwhile, Lannes's V Corps and part of the cavalry would keep the Russian right in play near the Santon. Hidden behind the Zurlan were the French reserves - perhaps twenty-two thousand men - the Imperial Guard, Bernadotte's troops, Oudinot's division and the rest of the cavalry, ready to exploit success. In all, 139 guns were in position.

The enemy played exactly into Napoleon's hands. Early on 2 December, in dense fog, Buxhowden led forward forty thousand Allies, in four columns, off the Pratzen and down into the shrouded valley near Telnitz and Sokolnitz, with a fifth force, another sixteen thousand strong, waiting under Kollowrath to follow them. Faced by such numbers, General Legrand was forced to give ground, but Davout's leading division enabled him to hold on. Napoleon, meanwhile was positioned atop the Zurlan, out of the fog, carefully studying the distant Pratzen. At nine o'clock he was satisfied the Allied centre was well-nigh bare of troops. The signal was given, and Vandamme's and St Hilaire's divisions swept up out of the fog to storm the Pratzen Heights. Too late, Kutusov tried to recall his out-sized left wing, and by midday, after some stiff fighting, Soult had secured control of the key height. On the French left, meanwhile, Lannes and Murat had fought off Bagration's thirteen thousand infantry and defeated Prince Lichtenstein's five thousand cavalry around the Santon and the hamlet of Bläswitz, and Davout and Legrand, after giving a little more ground on the right, had

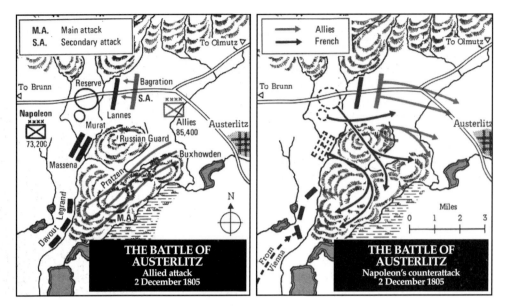

THE BATTLE OF
AUSTERLITZ
Allied attack
2 December 1805

THE BATTLE OF
AUSTERLITZ
Napoleon's counterattack
2 December 1805

stabilised their front as well, aided by Oudinot, sent south from the reserve.

In mounting confusion and despair, the Allies launched the Russian Imperial Guard - their last reserve - in a desperate attempt to retake the summit. Falling upon Vandamme's tired troops shortly after 1 pm, these picked soldiers made some progress but were then decisively counter-attacked by the Guard cavalry and part of Bernadotte's I Corps. The time had arrived for Napoleon's *coup de grâce*. Massing his reserves on the Pratzen, he ordered Soult to swing south. Soon Buxhowden's wing was trapped between the hills, the Goldbach and the frozen meres, and under attack from three sides. Trying to slip out of the trap, he managed to withdraw one column to the east; then, trying to save another, he ordered the men to scatter over the ice. French guns, ordered up by Napoleon, pulverised the surface, and over two thousand Austrians and some thirty guns sank to the bottom of the meres. Davout swept in from the west, issuing the grim order 'Let no one escape', and by 4 pm the destruction of the Allied left was almost complete. By this time, the Tsar and the Emperor Francis were leaving the field with the remnant of their Guards, and Bagration similarly headed back towards Olmütz.

Napoleon had won the great battle of Austerlitz, and in doing so had completely reversed the strategic position. For the loss of some nine thousand men, he had killed fifteen thousand Allies and taken eleven thousand prisoners, besides 180 cannon and forty-five colours. Even more important, he had broken the enemy will to resist further. On 3 December the Emperor Francis sued for peace, and the Tsar lost no time in heading back towards Poland. Thus, the Third Coalition, in its turn, lay in ruins, and Napoleon's new Empire had emerged triumphantly from the acid test of battle. By the Treaty of Pressburg, signed on 26 December, Austria ceded Venice, the Tyrol and Swabia to France and her German allies, Bavaria and Württemberg.

Pitt was prostrated by the news of this new disaster, and died in the New Year of 1806. Frederick William III of Prussia, so near to joining the Allies himself, hastened to send an envoy to Napoleon with a letter of congratulation on his victory. The Emperor was not fooled, remarking acidly to the envoy that the letter seemed to have been re-drafted. He was perfectly aware of Prussia's earlier intentions, and was not going to forget them. An account remained to be settled.

On 3 December 1805, the day after Austerlitz, the Emperor Francis II of Austria visited Napoleon to sue for an armistice. The Third Coalition lay in ruins.

The news of Austerlitz was received ecstatically in France and Napoleon's popularity reached new heights. Early hopes that a lasting peace would result from the triumph proved ill-founded, however, as Great Britain remained doggedly in the struggle, and Russia did not agree to a formal treaty. Napoleon, moreover, was not finished. He lost no time in exploiting his success by seizing Naples, and then turned his attention to reordering German affairs. In July 1806 the diffuse and anachronistic Holy Roman Empire was formally abolished - a further humiliation for Austria, and to fill the power-vacuum in central and western Germany Napoleon created the Confederation of the Rhine - basically a grouping of pro-French princelings.

The reforms which he introduced into the Confederation were resented and feared in nearby Prussia, but Napoleon was in a position to bully the weak-willed Frederick William III, and lost no opportunity of doing so. His power seemed limitless. Brother Joseph was appointed King of Naples; stepson Eugéne Beauharnais was made Viceroy of Italy; the loyal ruler of Bavaria was elevated to a throne; Louis Bonaparte became King of Holland.

Napoleon still retained some lingering hopes of reaching an agreement with Great Britain. As an olive branch, in June 1806 Napoleon suddenly offered to return the electorate of Hanover to George III. Only months earlier he had awarded Hanover to Prussia, in compensation for ceded territory along the Rhine, and this *volte-face* caused Prussia's smouldering resentment to burst into flame. On 7 August, driven by the strong-willed Queen Louise, the King and his vacillating government secretly decided on war against France, encouraged by promises of immediate aid from the Tsar. For once a secret was kept, and it was only in September, when Prussian preparations were well-advanced, that Napoleon learned what was in the wind. At his disposal were some 160,000 men, most of them veterans of the previous campaign, stationed from the Danube to the Main, but the Emperor did not at this stage discount the prowess of the Prussian army, which was capable of putting perhaps 170,000 troops in the field; he recalled and revered the memory of that army's creator, Frederick the Great, and his martial achievements. However, since Frederick's death, his army had mouldered under ageing generals, its regiments subject to endless ministerial red-tape, its officers over-confident and idle. Of the

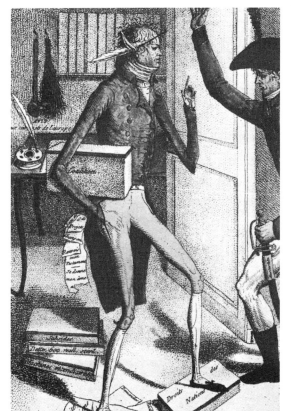

executive generals, Blücher was among the youngest, and he was already sixty-four years old. The senior commanders ranged up to eighty years of age, and this gerontocracy was not going to prove very successful against Napoleon and his energetic young marshals.

Only when news arrived on 18 September that Prussia had invaded Saxony, and that Russia had finally rejected France's offer of a treaty, did Napoleon take the omens seriously. Realising that these developments could only foreshadow the formation of a new coalition against him,

A French cartoon shows 'pen-pusher' William Pitt, his coalition schemes in ruins, confronted by Napoleon. The British premier died soon after Austerlitz.

Napoleon at once alerted his forces, issuing no fewer than 102 letters of instructions in a thirty-six-hour period (18-19 September). Reassured that Austria was in no condition to take the field, the Emperor debated three possible plans of campaign, his aim being to destroy the Prussian army before the Russians could intervene. By the 19th he had made his choice - a daring advance on Berlin itself through Saxony, despite the problems posed by the Thüringerwald area which would have to be traversed over three unconnected roads at the outset of the campaign. However, fully confident in the fighting qualities and flexibility of his army corps, Napoleon proceeded to divide his army into three columns for the crossing, trusting that surprise and speed, together with a feint offensive to be mounted by Louis Bonaparte over the Rhine, would see his army over the worst area before the Prussians could react in force. On 2 October, Napoleon formally assumed command of the army from Berthier at Würzburg - the very day

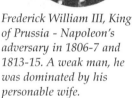

Frederick William III, King of Prussia - Napoleon's adversary in 1806-7 and 1813-15. A weak man, he was dominated by his personable wife.

Prussia presented an ultimatum in Paris. Napoleon's reply would be the invasion of Saxony six days later.

Although the die was cast, the Prussian commanders, Brunswick, Hohenlohe and Rüchel all held very discordant views on the best strategy to adopt. Eventually they settled for a drive on Stuttgart, designed to sever the links with France of the *Grande Armée*, supposedly still in quarters; but this plan was soon to be overtaken by events and abandoned. Confusion, not purpose, dominated the councils of the Prussian armies.

On 8 October, Napoleon's army entered Saxony in three columns, forty-one thousand, seventy thousand and fifty thousand strong, moving through Coburg, Kronach and Bayreuth respectively. The Thüringerwald was crossed, and on the 9th, Bernadotte and Murat (leading the central column) defeated a Prussian detachment under General Tauenzien at Schleiz, and next day Lannes repulsed Prince Louis Ferdinand at Rudolstadt. By the end of the 10th, the French army had reached the River Saale, while Hohenlohe tried to regroup his thirty-five thousand men near Jena, and Brunswick and Rüchel massed at Weimar to the west of the River Ilm. All were shocked by the sudden impact of the French offensive, and already they had lost the initiative.

For several days Napoleon remained uncertain of the Prussian's, whereabouts and intentions, and ordered his army to march north-east towards Leipzig, adopting for this move the three-column, *bataillon carré* formation, which permitted maximum flexibility. French cavalry patrols, however, found no sign of the foe between Gera and Leipzig, and Napoleon ordered his left wing to investigate the situation to the west, and Soult to remain near the River Elster in case the enemy were massing to the east. Then vital news came in from Lannes: the enemy was on his sector west of the Saale. Napoleon at once rode off to join V Corps just beyond Jena, ordering the whole army to march for the Saale, and indicating that he expected a major battle to take place near Weimar on or about the 16th. With complete precision, his flexible formation adjusted itself to the new direction.

After joining Lannes on the Landgrafenberg to the west of Jena during the evening of the 13th, Napoleon soon came to believe that the whole Prussian army was much closer than he had thought, and that in consequence the battle would take place on the 14th. At once new orders were despatched to the converging forces. Most formations were summoned to Jena, but Davout's III and Bernadotte's I Corps were to cross the Saale through Naumburg farther north (or, in the event of the I Corps not being in contact with the IIIrd, it was to move through Dornburg to the south) in order to sever the Prussian communications with Halle, the Elbe and distant Berlin. In fact, however, Napoleon was only partly correct in his calculations: only Hohenlohe's thirty-eight thousand men were close to Jena; Rüchel's thirteen thousand were still near Weimar, and the remaining fifty thousand were already moving north towards Auerstadt *en route* for Halle. This miscalculation, together with Bernadotte's deliberate misinterpretation of his orders, would place Davout's twenty-seven thousand men in an apparently impossible situation on the 14th.

By dawn, the Emperor had issued his plan. He envisaged a preliminary operation to secure the plateau below the Landgrafenberg to gain space for the formations still marching on Jena as they passed over the Saale, while Soult's and Augereau's corps carried out outflanking movements to the north and south respectively. Then, once he was strong enough, Napoleon planned to smash through the Prussian centre, and time his breakthrough to coincide with Davout's and Bernadotte's arrival in the Prussian rear.

In the event, matters worked out considerably differently.

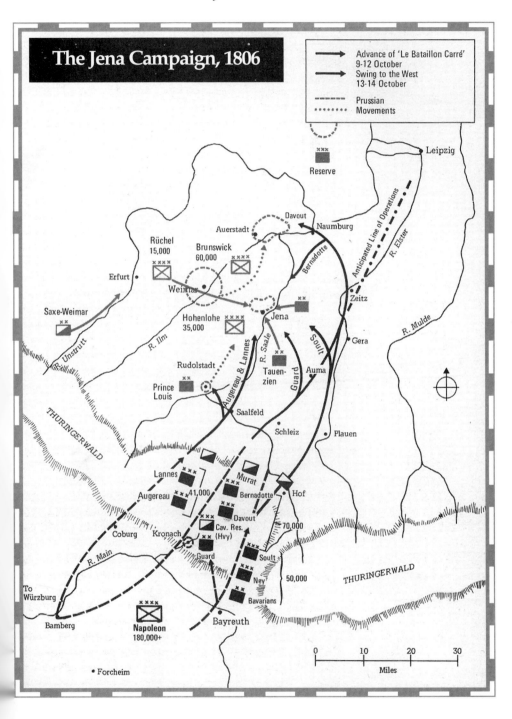

The Jena Campaign, 1806

→	Advance of 'Le Bataillon Carré' 9-12 October
→	Swing to the West 13-14 October
– – –	Prussian
• • • •	Movements

Reserve

Leipzig

R. Elster

Anticipated Line of Operations

Davout   Naumburg

Auerstadt

Rüchel 15,000

Brunswick 60,000

Erfurt

Weimar

Bernadotte

Zeitz

R. Mulde

Saxe-Weimar

Hohenlohe 35,000

Jena

Gera

R. Ilm

R. Saale

Soult

R. Unstrutt

Rudolstadt

Augereau & Lannes

Guard

Auma

THURINGERWALD

Prince Louis

Tauen- zien

Saalfeld

Schleiz

Plauen

Lannes

Murat

R. Main

Augereau   41,000

Bernadotte

Hof

Coburg   Kronach

Davout Cav. Res. (Hvy)

70,000

Guard

Soult

THURINGERWALD

To Würzburg

Ney   50,000

Bavarians

Bamberg

Napoleon 180,000+

Bayreuth

• Forcheim

0	10	20	30

Miles

Although the first parts of the plan were implemented by 10 am, the premature attack by Ney at the head of part of his corps led to a crisis in the centre that took some time to overcome. By 12.30 pm, however, Napoleon had ninety-six thousand men in the field, and although there was still no sign of Davout or Bernadotte, the Emperor decided that the time for the decisive central blow had come. Hohenlohe's battered and outnumbered battalions proved incapable of withstanding the relentless advance, and soon the Prussians were scattering. This fate was shared by Rüchel's contingents when they belatedly arrived from Weimar about 1pm. All was over by 3 pm, and an hour later Prince Murat was leading the French cavalry into Weimar. The French had lost five thousand men, but had inflicted casualties perhaps five times greater.

The Emperor's belief that he had routed the main Prussian army was rudely shattered when news at last arrived from the III Corps. Napoleon now learned that Davout had spent the day fighting and beating the major Prussian force of the King and Brunswick outside Auerstädt - accepting odds of two to one. Thick early morning mist had disguised the true weakness of the French on this secondary battlefield, and thereafter a combination of French valour and Prussian confusion, and not a few missed opportunities, had resulted in a dazzling success for Davout. The cost had been heavy: over seven thousand French officers and men out of the twenty-seven thousand engaged became casualties, but they accounted for thirteen thousand Prussians and induced the enemy to retreat for Halle.

There still remained the absence of the I Corps from both battlefields to explain. Had Bernadotte obeyed his orders and supported Davout, Auerstadt must have been a decisive success. However, the prickly Gascon, unwilling to take instructions from a colleague, had used a slight ambiguity in Napoleon's orders and marched his men away from Davout towards Dornbourg, and in the end had made no contribution to either battle. The Emperor's wrath was terrible, but Bernadotte escaped courtmartial by a hairsbreadth owing to the effective pursuit which his fresh troops led during the following days.

The pursuit after Jena was a military classic. Napoleon allowed his opponents no rest. On 16 October, Murat captured fourteen thousand disconsolate Prussians at Erfurt. Next day, Bernadotte won a sharp action at Halle, inflicting five thousand casualties. By the 20th the French were on the Elbe, as Hohenlohe broke away from his fellows and headed for Stettin. The 22nd saw the French

The coup d' état of 18 Brumaire almost ended in Bonaparte's lynching: he had to be rescued from the enraged Deputies by his troops. Detail from the painting by Bouchet.

The first sign of disillusion with Napoleon's seemingly ceaseless wars. A deputation from the French Senate waited upon the Emperor at the Royal Palace in Berlin soon after Jena-Auerstädt, and begged him to bring about a general pacification. The Emperor was affronted by this request, and it proved a pious hope.

over the Elbe at two places, and Ney commenced the siege of Magdeburg. On the 25th, Marshal Davout marched into Berlin, while two corps swung towards the River Oder to block any possible Russian intervention. Still, Prussian surrenders mounted. Hohenlohe gave up his sword to Murat at Prenzlau, along with another fourteen thousand men, on the 28th, and the dramatic month closed with the tame capitulation of the great fortress of Stettin, providing five thousand more prisoners, to a small force of bluffing French cavalry led by General Lasalle.

Of the Prussian field forces only Blücher remained, but on 6 November his force of twenty-two thousand laid down its arms to Bernadotte at Lübeck, a fate shared by a disembarking Swedish division - arrived too late to participate in this whirlwind campaign. Finally, on 10 November, the twenty-two thousand Prussians taking shelter within Magdeburg surrendered to Ney,

while Mortier took possession of Hamburg. Thus, in less than a calendar month, Napoleon and his lieutenants had accounted for all of 125,000 out of the original 160,000 Prussian troops in the field. Prussia had been brought to her knees. King Frederick William was a fugitive seeking safety in east Prussia, and not a Russian solder had yet entered the fray. It all amounted to an impressive achievement; never had the meaning of Napoleonic *blitzkrieg* been more convincingly demonstrated, and rarely had a military power been reduced to impotence more rapidly or effectively.

Yet Jena and Auerstadt did not bring peace. Prussia might have been humiliatingly defeated, but the Tsar's forces had still to be encountered, and Russian assurances of immediate aid fortified Frederick William's shaky resolve to remain in the war for a further period. To this extent, therefore the campaign of 1806 had an unsatisfactory conclusion. The Fourth Coalition still remained in being, and, as always, British hostility remained unshakeable.

The immediate problem facing Napoleon in late 1806 was twofold: to force Prussia to make peace, and to defeat the Russian armies of the Tsar. The approach of winter was a major complication, but in the hope of snatching a quick success against Generals Kamenskoi, Bennigsen and Buxhowden, he decided to advance deep into Polish territory, at that time largely parcelled up between Prussia and Russia. There was also a possibility of attracting recruits for his armies, for Polish patriots had long dreamed of regaining a semblance of independence for their historic nation. By mid-November the French were half-way to Warsaw, and on the 28th Murat occupied the Polish capital unopposed.

At this juncture, the French paused to reorder their dispositions in the hope that the Russians would blunder into a trap. Napoleon planned to advance on Pultusk where Russian communications crossed the River Narew, while Bernadotte and Ney pushed from Thorn to Beizun and the River Ukra to cut the Russians off from

Napoleon ordered his army into the Alpine passes. The gun-barrels had to be placed on extemporised sledges (made from split tree-trunks) to overcome the ice and snow at the head of the Great St Bernard Pass-the route used by the main column in May 1800. Note the field-forge.

east Prussia. The Russians duly massed at Pultusk, and in mid-December the French Emperor launched his corps forward. The next weeks saw a number of combats and manoeuvres around the River Narew, but the French failed to force a major battle, and became over-extended, and the Russians were able to extricate their forces. By early January 1807, Kamenskoi had made good his escape, and the French offensive ground to a halt. 'The terrible roads and bad weather have persuaded me to enter winter quarters', wrote Napoleon.

The corps were dispersed over French-occupied Poland, and made what provisions they could against the bitter weather. They were not, however, to be long rested. In late January, Marshal Ney decided to move his starving troops to a more comfortable region. In mid-journey northwards, be brushed with a large Russian force which was advancing to attempt a surprise attack on Bernadotte's I Corps at Mohringen. The news was rushed to Napoleon at Warsaw, where he was passing the weeks snugly enough with Marie Walewska, his current mistress. The Emperor at once ordered the whole army into the field despite the intemperate season: Bernadotte was ordered to withdraw westwards and lure the enemy after him, and Ney to draw closer to the main army, which was marching to trap the Russians near Inkovo.

The charming Polish Countess Marie Walewska. She proved the most loyal of Napoleon's many mistresses, visiting him in exile on Elba 1814.

Fate abruptly took a hand. One copy of Bernadotte's orders fell into Russian hands, and warned Bennigsen of his peril. At once the Russians began to fall back on Allenstein. 'It is now clear that he appreciates our manoeuvres... and wishes to escape', commented Napoleon. As a result, the engagement of Allenstein on 3 February was indecisive, and the Russians fell back towards Eylau, abandoning depots at Güttstadt and Liebstadt to the hungry French, still in full pursuit.

Bennigsen now determined to halt and face his enemy. He had sixty-seven thousand troops and all of 470 guns, and was hopeful that the Prussian Lestocq, currently shadowing Ney with perhaps ten thousand men, would join him in time for the battle. Thus on 7

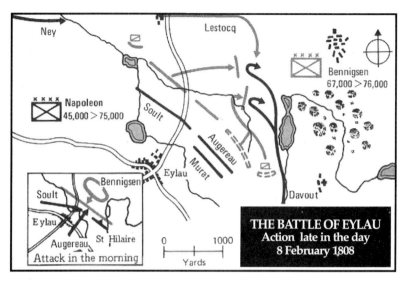

February when Napoleon's forces at last encountered the Russians in the late afternoon and ultimately drove them out of Eylau village itself, the French numbered only forty-five thousand men and 210 guns. Both Davout and Ney were still far from the battle area, numbering perhaps thirty thousand more men between them, but Napoleon hoped also that Bernadotte would come up in time. In fact this was impossible, as the commander of the I Corps had received no orders.

After a bitter night, the two armies took up battle positions separated by a frozen plain. The French position was centred around Eylau and Rothenen villages, and extended along a low ridge. The Russians were drawn up around Anklappen to the north-east and had made unavailing attempts - given the hardness of the earth - to entrench their front. The Russian cannon opened the struggle with a sustained bombardment, but Napoleon bided his time, hoping that Davout, Ney and Bernadotte would come up before he launched his attack. The Marshals were under orders to turn the Russian left and right respectively, but there was still no sign of them at 9 am, and Russian pressure against Soult's corps on Napoleon's left was becoming serious. In an attempt to cause a distraction, the Emperor ordered Augereau to lead his VII Corps in an attack on the Russian left, supported by St Hilaire's division. Unfortunately this coincided with a heavy snowstorm, and the two French forces became separated. Lost in the blizzard, Augereau's corps veered towards the Russian centre where it was pulverised by the massed Russian artillery. The corps was shattered, and St Hilaire was too weak to break through on his own.

Napoleon soon found the situation deteriorating even further. A Russian counter-attack reached his command-post in Eylau before being repulsed, and the Emperor was saved from death or capture only by the devotion of his staff. In a desperate attempt to conceal the critical weakness of his own centre, Napoleon ordered Prince Murat to charge with all his 10,700 cavalry and repel the looming Russian columns. All of eighty squadrons were in the first wave.

The celebrated charge that ensued was successful beyond all expectation. Murat's horsemen, massed in two vast columns, crashed right through both Russian lines, rallied into single column and then took the enemy gunners in the rear before they could re-align. This success won a breathing space, and Davout arrived at last from the south-east. From 1 pm the newcomers slowly but remorselessly pressed back the Russian left until it was placed at right angles to the centre. But still there was no sign of Ney on the farther flank and the arrival of the Prussian Lestocq (who had eluded the VI Corps) from the north, enabled Bennigsen to reinforce his left in the nick of time. Step by step, the III Corps was forced back in its turn until the front was almost re-established along its original line.

Only at 7 pm, when dusk had already fallen, did Ney make his tardy appearance. It was too late to use the VI Corps for anything more than a demonstration, but it sufficed to persuade the Russian high command to abandon its plans for renewing the conflict the following day. This was a relief to the French, who had fought to a standstill amid atrocious conditions. Napoleon took pains to disguise his losses, but they may have been in excess of twenty thousand men; the Russians lost perhaps fifteen thousand men. Both sides claimed a victory, but there was no disguising that for the first time in his career Napoleon had failed to win a decisive battle. Furthermore, the problem of defeating the Russians still remained, as they had retreated in good order on Königsberg. There was scant attempt at pursuit, and soon the exhausted French were gratefully returning into their winter quarters. So ended the indecisive winter campaign of 1806-7. Napoleon vented his wrath on Bernadotte, in this case wholly unjustly. If anyone had bungled the battle of Eylau, it was the Emperor himself, who had summoned Ney to the field far too late. The fate of the campaign, therefore, was undecided, and would wait through the harsh winter until warm summer made further operations possible.

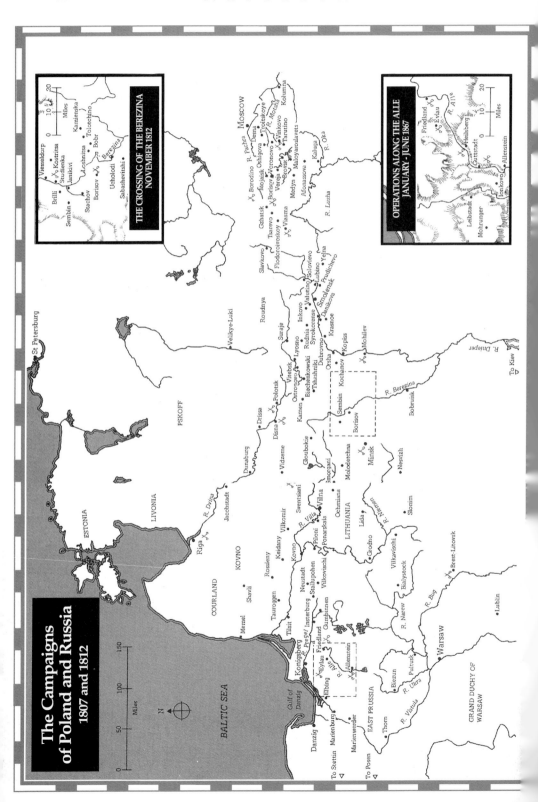

THE CROSSING OF THE BEREZINA NOVEMBER 1812

Vesseldorp
Brilli
Kostritsa
Studienka
Janikivi
Kamienska
Tolotchino
Bobr
Loshnitsa
Stachov
Borisov
Ucholodi
Sabashevitshi
Sembin
Berezina

OPERATIONS ALONG THE ALLE JANUARY - JUNE 1867

Friedland
Eylau
Heilsberg
R. Alle
Guttstadt
Liebstadt
Mohrungen
Tonkovo
Allenstein

MOSCOW
R. Pachra
Desna
R. Moja
Troitskoye
Borodino
Mojaisk
Oshigova
Voronovo
Vinkovo
Kolumna
Tarutino
Vereja
Medyn
Bosvk
Maloyaroslavets
Afonassova
Kaluga
R. Oka
R. Lusha

Gzhatsk
Tarevo
Viasma
Flodorovosksy
Slavkovo
Lubino
Solovievo
Valutino
Yelna
Inkovo
Prudichevo
Rudnia
Smolensk
Ostrowno
Syrokorense
Danikova
Lyosno
Tbashtniki
Dubrovno
Krasnoe
Kamen
Bieschenkowki
Orsha
Kopiss
Vitebsk
Mohilev
Suraje
Roudnia

St Petersburg

Velikye-Luki

PSKOFF

Polotsk
Drissa
Disna
Videme
Gloubokie
Kochanov
Sembin
Borisov
R. Berezina
Bobruisk

Dunaburg

LIVONIA
R. Dvina
Jacobstadt
Riga

ESTONIA

Smorgani
Molodetchna
Minsk
Nesvizh

KOVNO
Rossieny
Keidany
Vilkomir
Kovno
Swientsiani
Vilna
Ochmiana
Ponarskaja
R. Vilia
Piloni
LITHUANIA
Lida
Slonim
Grodno
R. Niemen

COURLAND
Shavli
Memel
Taurogen
Tilsit
Neustadt
Stalluponen
Gumbinnen
Vilkovischi
Vilkovischi
Bialystock
Brest-Litovsk

Konigsberg
R. Pregel
Interburg
Friedland
Eylau
Allenstein
EAST PRUSSIA
Biezun
Pultusk
R. Ukra

BALTIC SEA
N
Gulf of Danzig
Danzig
Marienburg
Marienwerder
To Stettin
To Posen
Elbing
Thorn

R. Bug
R. Narew
R. Vistula
Warsaw
Lublin
GRAND DUCHY OF WARSAW

Miles
0   50   100   150

The Campaigns of Poland and Russia 1807 and 1812

To Kiev
R. Dnieper

Napoleon's enemies had no intention of allowing him long to recover. Nor had the Emperor any intention of withdrawing. New drafts for the French army were hastily rushed from recruiting depots to make good as much of the damage sustained as possible. And on 26 April Prussia and Russia signed a new agreement at Bartens re-affirming their determination to remain in the field - 1807 would be a decisive year. Meanwhile, Lefebvre besieged and captured Danzig (27 May).

Early in June, under heavy pressure from St Petersburg, Bennigsen resumed the offensive and set out to isolate Napoleon from the Baltic. Once he realised what was happening, Napoleon rushed his troops northwards, intent on cutting enemy communications with Königsberg. Between 8 and 10 June, the French fought two actions against parts of the Russian army at Güttstadt and Heilsberg respectively. Alerted by these checks, Bennigsen retreated up the east bank of the River Alle until he reached Friedland, where he turned at bay on the 13th, starting to cross, most unwisely, to the west bank - thus placing the river to his back. The reason for this extraordinary action was the chance to engage an apparently isolated French *corps d'armée*, that of Lannes. But as usual, appearances could be highly deceptive and soon Napoleon had neighbouring forces hastening towards Benningsen's fifty-three thousand men of whom twelve thousand were kept on the right bank of the Alle in wasteful detachments. The Emperor was ready for the battle of Friedland.

The first actions took place at dawn, when Lannes, reinforced by Grouchy's cavalry to a strength of twelve thousand men, took

The battle of Eylau, 8 February 1807. Outnumbered, Napoleon almost lost this battle, fought amid appalling winter weather conditions, but at the crisis of the day, Prince Murat led a superb cavalry charge which halted the Russian advance, and won time for the French reserves to arrive. The battle ended in a draw, but the French held the field.

The eve of Austerlitz, 1 December 1805, by General Lejuene. Napoleon questions peasants about the movements of the Russo-Austrian army. In the background is the Santon Hill. Detail from the painting at Versailles.

A romanticised representation of the meeting of Queen Louise and Napoleon at Tilsit in July 1807. The Queen of Prussia tried every feminine wile to get more favorable terms for her country, but failed. She was the consort of King Frederick William III, and was described by Napoleon as 'The only real man in Prussia'.

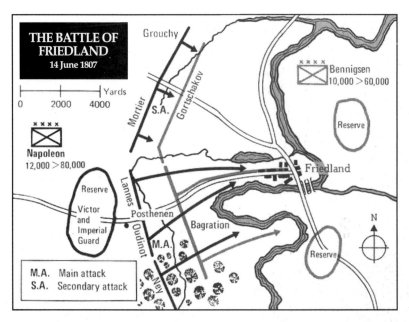

THE BATTLE OF
FRIEDLAND
14 June 1807

Yards
0   2000   4000

Napoleon
12,000 > 80,000

Grouchy

Gortschakov

Mortier

S.A.

Bennigsen
10,000 > 60,000

Reserve

Reserve

Lannes

Victor
and
Imperial
Guard

Posthenen

Oudinot

Bagration

Friedland

N

M.A.

Ney

Reserve

M.A.   Main attack
S.A.   Secondary attack

control of the hamlet of Posthenen two miles west of Friedland.
Skirmishing continued until 9 am, by which time French strength
had grown to all of seventeen thousand, and that of Bennigsen to
forty-five thousand. Russian troops were still pouring over the
pontoon bridges, but their generals did not press their numerical
advantage, remaining largely passive. By 10 am, the French had
over forty thousand in the field, and at midday Napoleon arrived
to take over command. Davout, Soult and Murat had still to come
up, and his staff advised the Emperor to delay the main battle until
the 15th, but by 4 pm, the Guard and most of the I Corps had made
their appearance, bringing the French to eighty thousand men. Not
only did the Russians have the Alle to their rear, but their four-mile
battle-line was bisected by the Millstream. 'We cannot hope to
surprise the enemy making the same mistake twice', Napoleon
concluded, and decided to attack without delay. His plan was this:
Oudinot's corps was to make a provocative movement from the
right centre, while Lannes and Mortier held the centre and left
respectively. Then, when the moment came, Ney's corps was to
sweep in against the two Russian divisions south of the Millstream,
and roll up the Russian left upon the centre, while the massed
French cavalry waited to turn defeat into rout. General Victor's
corps and the Imperial Guard were kept in central reserve.

The capitulations of Madrid on 4 December 1808, five months after the French disaster at Bailen. Napoleon is shown receiving a delegation of hidalgos, come to surrender the city.

At 5.30 pm, a twenty-gun battery gave the signal for Ney to advance from the cover of Sortlach Wood to the south. This move astonished Bennigsen, who had not expected action at this late hour, and he was forced to cancel a newly-issued order for his army to withdraw over the Alle. He at once despatched a force of Cossacks and regular cavalry to intercept Ney's advance, but this move was countered by Latour-Maubourg at the head of the French right-wing cavalry.

Ney's advance continued despite considerable losses, and the Russian left began to give ground. At a critical moment, Napoleon sent Victor to reinforce Ney's battered left wing, and this enabled the VI Corps to maintain its impetus. The Russian Bagration, commanding the left, was forced back in growing chaos towards Friedland, Dupont's division and Brigadier-General Sénarmont's thirty guns, deployed well forward, allowing the enemy no respite. Russian cavalry was flung in to retrieve the situation, only to be massacred by point-blank case-shot in their turn. About 7 pm,

The storm of Ratisbon 23 April 1809. Painting by Thevenin at Versailles. Marshal Lannes enouraged the assault party. The Austrian army was defeated. During the engagement Napoleon was slightly wounded when a bullet grazed his right heel.

Bennigsen committed the Russian Imperial Guard on the left, and ordered Gortschakov to attack the French left and centre as a diversion, but neither of these moves succeeded. Lannes and Mortier stood their ground and Ney and Dupont defeated the Russian Imperial Guard. By 8 pm, the Russian left and centre was being crowded back into Freidland itself, with only a single bridge still intact behind them.

Within half an hour Ney's troops were in possession of half the town and the time was ripe for Grouchy's massed squadrons on the far left to destroy the Russian right. This attack was, however, badly bungled, and the Russians were fortunate enough to discover a number of fords over the Alle which enabled much of their right and centre to make good their escape, covered by the fire of the Russian reserve manning the east bank.

*The celebrated summit meeting
between the two emperors on the
raft moored in the River Niemen
near Tilsit. Superficially, the
agreements reached at this
conference in July 1807 brought
Napoleon to the summit of his
power.*

Nevertheless, Napoleon had won a decisive victory. For a loss of
eight thousand casualties he had inflicted almost twenty thousand
on the Russians, and captured eighty of their 130 cannon.
Retreating through Allenburg, Bennigsen strove to reorder his
demoralised army, but the fall of Königsberg to Soult on the 16th
deprived the Russians of their depots, and by the 19th, Murat's
cavalry had reached the Niemen near Tilsit. The Tsar promptly sued
for an armistice, and on 23 June a four-week cessation of hostilities
became effective. Well might Napoleon declare: 'My children have
worthily celebrated the anniversary of Marengo.' The set-back at
Eylau had been avenged, and everything now pointed to a
favourable peace with Russia.

Tsar Alexander and Emperor Napoleon met on the famous raft anchored in mid-stream of the Niemen on 25 June 1807. During the two weeks of negotiations that followed, Napoleon lost no opportunity to dazzle and impress Alexander, but behind the façade of reviews and banquets, hard bargaining was taking place. Inevitably, the only real victim was unfortunate Prussia. Frederick William was summoned to attend the conferences, and despite Queen Louise, who tried every feminine wile to get more favourable terms, Prussia was virtually dismembered. By the treaty ratified on 12 July, Prussia was returned to her frontiers of 1772. All possessions west of the Elbe were to be incorporated into a new kingdom of Westphalia (to be ruled by Jerome Bonaparte), and all Prussia's Polish provinces were incorporated into the new grand duchy of Warsaw. Prussia's army was to be restricted, and a huge war indemnity to be paid. Pending the fulfilment of these terms, French troops would remain in occupation of Prussian soil. Russia, predictably, came off more lightly. In return for the Tsar's cession of the Ionian Isles, Napoleon agreed to Russian claims for freedom of action against European Turkey and Finland. Alexander also agreed to join the Continental System, and to induce Sweden and Denmark to follow suit. Recognition was accorded to Joseph as King of Naples, Louis as King of Holland and Jerome as King of Westphalia, while the rulers of Bavaria and Saxony were also to receive crowns. Thus, the two potentates agreed to a virtual partition of continental Europe between them.

Napoleon's triumph appeared complete. His international prestige seemed to have reached new height and his power extended ostensibly from the Pyrenees to the Nieman. However, these magnificent appearances concealed weaknesses. The Continental System was already highly unpopular in western Europe, as was the 'blood-tax' of conscription and the heavy incidence of taxation. In France itself there were murmurs against the extension of Napoleon's ambitions to European dimensions.

His popularity, therefore, was brittle. As for the *Grande Armée*, although it had re-established its reputation at Friedland, its composition was no longer exclusively French, but becoming increasingly multi-national. There was friction between the marshals, the line troops distrusted the staff, and the infantry was critical of the cavalry. If Tilsit has been widely regarded as the highwater mark of the First French Empire, it would also prove to be the turn of the tide.

The spread of the family caucus. Following Tilsit, European royalty was soon taking on a decidedly Napoleonic aspect. Three of the Emperor's brothers received crowns, as did his brother-in-law, Joachim Murat. His stepson, Eugène, became Viceroy of Italy.

CHAPTER FOUR

The Path to Failure
1808-12

In the space of a few brief years, Napoleon had destroyed successively the armies of Russia, Prussia and Austria, but there remained Great Britain, hostile and implacable across the Channel, protected by the supremacy of the Royal Navy. Napoleon had long abandoned the idea of invasion, and had turned instead to a new tactic - to subdue her through blockade.

The Continental System, as it was called, was simple. It had come into being shortly after Jena, and consisted of an embargo on British trade with the European territories dominated by France. With each successive victory, the embargo was written into the peace treaties: it was extended, moreover, to European neutrals who were told that trading with Britain would be regarded as a hostile act. As a scheme, it was a good one; as a practical proposition, it both proved ineffective and, indeed, rebounded on its inventor. For Britain, after all, traded not only with Europe but with a far-flung Empire unchallengeable while she held command of the seas. She demonstrated her power by forbidding seaborne trade with France

The crossing of the Beresina, November 1812 - as depicted by an unknown soldier, present at the scene. This success saved the remnants of the Grande Armée from complete destruction, but was achieved only at a terrible cost.

Joachim Murat, French marshal, Prince of Berg, imperial brother-in-law and, later, King of Naples. Married to Caroline Bonaparte, this cavalryman's advancement was indeed dramatic. A great leader of cavalry, famous for his elaborate uniforms, he lacked a broad grasp of both military strategy and diplomatic finesse. His adventurous life ended with his back to a wall in 1815.

in war materials and, in August 1807, took possession of the Danish fleet to prevent its falling into French hands. The blockade with England was difficult to enforce, and was bitterly resented by the European powers. Even Napoleon's own brother, Louis of Holland, defied the ruling and in 1810 was forced to abdicate because of it. Above all, as we shall see, the administration of the System forced Napoleon - for purely nominal advantages - into a number of decisions which seriously affected his European grand strategy.

But for the moment Napoleon had every reason for confidence and now set his sights on Portugal. Britain's oldest ally refused to subscribe to the Continental System, and if she fell to France the Royal Navy would be deprived of the use of the Tagus, and Portuguese ports - at home and in Brazil - would be closed to British trade. Accordingly, within a month of leaving Tilsit, Napoleon laid plans to overthrow Portugal's Regency government.

On 2 August the *Corps d'Observation de la Gironde* was formed under General Junot and by 16 October a second force was in readiness under Dupont. Merciless propaganda pressure was applied, and Spain was secretly induced to aid the forthcoming invasion with both facilities and troops. Early in November Junot stood poised at the head of twenty-five thousand men, not far from the Portuguese frontier, and French demands of Portugal became ever more strident.

On 16 November, Junot was ordered to advance. The crossing of the mountains along the frontier proved difficult, but two weeks later, Junot managed to reach Lisbon, against very feeble opposition, fulfilling to the letter Napoleon's order. However, he arrived at the head of only two thousand troops - the rest having fallen temporarily by the roadside - to find that the Regent had evacuated the capital, removing a great deal of treasure and the Portuguese fleet.

Napoleon and Godoy, the 'Prince of the Peace' and *de facto* manager of the Spanish government, set about partitioning Portugal, but the invaders were widely detested, and popular revolts soon broke out. Moreover, France-Spanish relations were far from easy, for Napoleon now had first-hand information on Spain's disregard of the Continental System. Holding Godoy, a sometime private soldier and now lover to the Spanish Queen, in total contempt, Napoleon secretly began to prepare for a French takeover of power in Spain. With key bases such as Valladolid, Burgos and Vitoria already partly in French hands, this was not expected to prove too difficult; three French corps were already in position, and on 16 February 1808, Murat was appointed the Emperor's Lieutenant in Spain. By the end of the month, subterfuge and minimal force had secured the French such key fortresses as Pamplona and Barcelona, and all was nearly ready.

Playing upon the known divisions within the Spanish royal family, Napoleon engineered a crisis. Fears for Charles IV's life (supposedly threatened by his son, Ferdinand) had induced the King to flee his capital, but a local rising trapped him at Aranjuez. Responding to Charles's urgent entreaties for French aid, Napoleon ordered Murat to march on Madrid. The capital was occupied on 13 March, and in the guise of mediator, he summoned the various parties to Bayonne in France in late April. There he showed his hand and Charles was compelled to abdicate in favour of Napoleon as 'caretaker', and his son was similarly bullied into renouncing his rights.

This bare-faced takeover was crowned on 10 May by the proclamation of Joseph Bonaparte as King of Spain, the vacant Neapolitan throne being awarded in due course to Murat. But the hostility provoked, not surprisingly, soon became apparent. As early as 1 April a minor rising occurred at Madrid, but those of 2 May were far more serious. Spanish loyalty to their Bourbon rulers proved unexpectedly strong and by the end of the month a wave of terror struck the country as Spanish collaborators and several Frenchmen were murdered in wide areas across the country. By 10 June all the Provinces were openly arming, and the French found

CHARLES IV. ET SA FAMILLE
remettent à l'Empereur tous leurs droits à la Couronne des Espagnes.

Tom.IV.

The Bayonne Conference, April 1808. Napoleon tricked and bullied the Spanish Bourbon royal family into relinquishing all rights to the throne. He would live to regret it, as the result was a national rising - the 'Spanish ulcer' - which the French never mastered, thanks to the presence of the British army in the Peninsula.

themselves with a truly national war on their hands. It is true that liberal elements among the Spanish aristocracy and *bourgeoisie* welcomed the change in power as the only means to free the state from corruption, the Inquisition and outdatedness; but the mass of the people were strongly opposed. At this juncture, Murat fell seriously ill and left for France on the 29th.

Even worse news was to follow. Napoleon ordered 'flying columns' to pacify the country, and Bessières, Moncey, Dupont and Duhesme set out to do their master's bidding. At this stage there were 120,000 French troops already in Spain. At first, progress seemed to be being maintained. Bessières defeated part of the Spanish royal army under General Cuesta at Rio Seco on 14 July, although Moncey failed to secure Valencia. Dupont, moving into Andalusia, occupied Cordoba, but was then induced to fall back to Bailen where, on 20 July, he surrendered three divisions to General Castaños. This news caused a great sensation in Spain and throughout Europe. The capitulation also unfortunately coincided with Joseph's first entry into his capital, hardly a happy omen for the new reign, and by 6 August the new King had abandoned Madrid and fallen back with most of his forces behind the River Douro.

At this juncture a new complication arose. Spanish appeals for British aid resulted in the arrival in Portugal of Sir Arthur Wellesley and fourteen thousand men. On 21 August this force decisively defeated Junot at Vimeiro and a convention was arranged at Cintra by Wellesley's newly-arrived superior, Sir Harry Burrard, whereby

Junot agreed to abandon Portugal. These set-backs led Napoleon to take two key decisions. The first was to summon Victor's, Mortier's and Ney's experienced corps from the Elbe. The second was to take command in Spain in person. On 7 September l'Armée d'Espagne was formally designated. But before he could leave for Spain, Napoleon had to secure himself in central Europe, especially as he was about to transfer one hundred thousand veteran troops to Spain, almost a third of his forces in Germany. Accordingly, on 27 September he met Tsar Alexander for two weeks of talks at Erfurt. The atmosphere was notably different from that at Tilsit. In return for vague promises to keep watch on Austria, whom Napoleon feared might take the opportunity to strike in his absence, the Tsar extracted the right to occupy Moldavia and Wallachia in the Balkans and also French acknowledgement of Russian gains in Finland. With this one-sided agreement Napoleon had to be content, and only time would show that his faith in Alexander was misplaced. The 'spirit of Tilsit' was already a dead letter, and Alexander, rather than Napoleon, had dominated the Congress.

The central *Junta* of Spain could call upon some two hundred thousand troops, many of indifferent quality, besides numbers of partisans. Their military leaders were unreliable, except possibly Blake and Palafox, but at the same time, the growing British army, thirty thousand strong and now commanded by Sir John Moore, following the recall of Burrand and Wellesley, was preparing to send twenty thousand men to co-operate with the Spanish authorities.

Yet Spanish plans were muddled and uncertain, and that would never be the case with Napoleon. By early November, the Emperor, his transfers complete, had two hundred thousand men massed behind the Ebro. Of these, over 160,000 were available for the great offensive. The plan envisaged an advance over the Ebro followed by two flank attacks making a double outward wheel through Logroño and Burgos respectively to encircle Blake to the north-west, and Palafox and Castaños to the east. Those armies eliminated, the road to Madrid would lie open.

The campaign proper opened on 7 November, though Lefebvre had attacked Blake against orders on 30 October near Durango, giving him the chance to fall back before the trap could be sprung. But the first stages were successful enough. Burgos was eventually seized by Soult on 10 November, following the dismissal of Bessiéres for tardiness, and next day Napoleon was able to resume the execution of the master plan. Victor, chastened by a minor setback to part of his force, was soon in hot pursuit of Blake, and Ney swung east to trap Castaños.

The problems posed by supply and the difficult terrain thwarted the French of complete success, but by the 23rd they had three minor victories to their credit, while Napoleon had forty-five thousand experienced troops massing around Aranda ready to head the dash for Madrid. Five days later, 130,000 men were on the move for the capital. Napoleon selected the Somosierra Pass for his crossing of the last mountains, and on the 30th forced his way through the nine thousand Spaniards trying to block the road, but only after causing heavy casualties to the Polish Light Horse by his insistence on premature and unsupported attacks. By midday on 4 December, the French were masters of the Retiro Heights, the central *Junta* had fled for Badajoz, and before dusk Madrid was in French hands.

Napoleon now believed that the conquest of Spain was all but achieved. As he regrouped his forces around Madrid preparatory to launching them southwards against the weak Spanish forces that still remained, only one uncertainty nagged him. What had happened to General Moore, of whose presence in Spain he had first heard in mid-November?

In fact, Moore was closer than the Emperor knew. After learning of the initial defeats of Blake and Castaños, the British general had considered an immediate retreat towards Lisbon, but had then decided to march to the aid of Blake's successor, General La Romana. He had in support five thousand recent reinforcements

The Somosierra Pass today, looking north from the Spanish position towards the French line of advance.

under General Baird, and, on 11 December, Moore advanced with a total of twenty-five thousand men from Salamanca. He struck at once for Sahagun in the hope of surprising Soult's II Corps in a scattered situation, though Soult reacted to this threat in time. But when the news reached Madrid on 19 December the effect was electric. All Napoleon's hatred for Britain burst forth, and he immediately cancelled his orders for an advance into the south of Spain, substituting an all-out attempt to trap and destroy

The battle of Somosierra, 30 November 1808. Advancing from Burgos, Napoleon faced only one major natural obstacle blocking his road to Madrid - the Somosierra Pass. The Emperor personally conducted the operation to capture it, but his patience snapped and he insisted on an unsupported cavalry attack which led to fearful losses. Eventually the pass was rescued by the French, and Madrid was occupied four days later.

Moore. Then, on the 21st, he hounded his men over the ice-bound Guadarrama Pass, ordering Soult to pin Moore until the main army could attack his flank and rear.

However, Moore was not going to be so obliging. As soon as he learned of Napoleon's move from Madrid, he ordered a headlong retreat over the mountains towards Corunna, where he requested the Royal Navy to make preparations for the evacuation of the army. A race developed through bitter weather, but Moore managed always to keep ahead of his pursuers, turning from time to time to engage their advance guard. Both armies suffered great

The pursuit of Moore's British army towards Corunna. Napoleon hounds his men over the ice-bound Guadarrama Pass, 21 December 1808, in the hope of catching the 'perfidious English'. He was disappointed.

distress during this period, but on 31 December Napoleon conceded that the British were likely to reach Corunna. He promptly handed over the pursuit to Soult, and began to divert superfluous formations back towards Madrid where Joseph, surrounded as he was by a hostile population, was desperate for troops. The Emperor was therefore not present at the battle of Corunna on 16 January 1809, where Moore, at the cost of his own life, repulsed Soult and won time for the evacuation of the remainder of his army.

It was never Napoleon's way to be associated personally with failure. He also had other reasons for turning away - for alarming news of plots in Paris came hard on the heels of intelligence reports that Austria was secretly mobilising on the Danube. So it was that on 6 January Napoleon left Astorga and headed for Valladolid on

what would prove the first stage of his return to France. Thus he left the Spanish theatre without completing the conquest he had set out to achieve. Moore's army might have been forced into a desperate retreat and evacuation from the mainland, but its commander had effectively ruined the French programme for the subjugation of southern Spain and Portugal; and before many months were out, the British army would have returned under Wellesley (later to become Duke of Wellington), ready to turn an already difficult situation for the French into an impossible one. For, although the regular Spanish forces were scattered, the will of the Spanish people was far from broken, and the guerrilla struggle, backed by the British army's presence, would make the 'Spanish ulcer' incurable for the French.

The Emperor himself was never to return to Spain - though Wellington was to record the view that 'If Boney had been here, we'd have been beat.' So, in the years that followed, the Peninsular War placed an increasing strain on French resources as they were being stretched in the continental campaigns to come. A succession of French marshals failed to bring victory, and Joseph was never more than a nominal ruler of a disaffected people, holding on uneasily, and far from enthusiastically, with the aid of French troops sorely needed elsewhere.

Meanwhile, far away in Vienna, the 'War Party' led by the Austrian Empress Ludovica was growing in influence. Francis II and all sections of his Court were equally keen to seek revenge for Austerlitz - the only point at issue being the question of timing. Those advocating immediate action argued that Napoleon's involvement with Spain and the absence of his key subordinates made the moment favourable. The reasoning was persuasive and on 8 February 1809 the decision for war was taken. The declaration would come two months later.

Since the humiliation at Austerlitz, the Austrian army had been transformed into a national army. The first-line strength had

General Sir John Moore, killed at Corunna, 16 January 1809. His bold decision saved southern Spain and Portugal from immediate French occupation.

In June 1809, they resorted to the Spanish method of garroting at Barcelona.

been raised to 350,000, supplemented by a *Landwehr* which would eventually total 240,000. Archduke Charles had copied the *corps d'armée* system, creating eleven corps in all; he revised the drill-book to include a form of skirmishing tactics, reorganised the cavalry, and increased the artillery to comprise 760 field guns. The senior commanders, however, Charles apart, remained rather stolid and uninspiring and the staff system continued to be defective. The Austrian plan for 1809, after various schemes had been considered, was to send only a holding force into north Italy, and to use eight corps for a mighty blow south of the Danube to destroy the French forces in the Ulm-Augsburg area, but first to capture Ratisbon, the vital link for the French with their forces in the Nuremberg-Bamberg area.

'The Horrors of War'

The guerrilla war which flared up all over Spain from May 1808, was fought with great bitterness on both sides. Atrocity and counter-attrocity were commonly committed. The French were not slow to execute Spanish patriots who fell into their hands.

Napoleon, back in Paris, was taking urgent measures to strengthen his army in Germany, which, thanks to Spain and the many garrison detachments needed there, could field barely 80,000 of its nominal 120,000 men; 110,000 men, due for conscription in 1810, were mobilised a whole year early; France's allies were abruptly notified that they should produce another 100,000 - for the Emperor required an army of 260,000 in Germany and 150,000 in Italy. Divisions were redesignated as corps, new officers were commissioned from the ranks and by late March the 174,000 men available in Germany were renamed *La Grande Armée de l'Allemagne*. By that date, taking all sectors outside Spain, Napoleon could deploy some 275,000 men against the Austrian Hapsburgs. This was far from his target, and quality was not particularly good, but he hoped to improve the situation before it came to open war. It was little wonder that he felt bitter at the Tsar's failure even to attempt to implement the Erfurt agreement.

Moreover, Austria was determined to strike the first blow. On 9 April, without formal declaration of war, the Austrian forces began to move, and within a day had invaded Bavaria. Berthier, in command of the French army in Napoleon's absence, was taken largely by surprise, and in bewilderment and in direct contravention of a paragraph in the Emperor's orders, decided to concentrate Davout, Oudinot and Lefebvre at Ratisbon - right in the path of the advancing enemy. This laid the French open to having

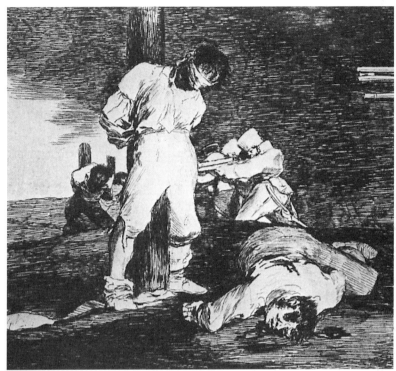

French reprisals continued to mount - as illustrated by the execution scene, also by Goya - but they never broke the spirit of the Spanish people. Napoleon came to rue his involvement in the Spanish Peninsula.

The ferocious hatred inspired by the French is well captured in this drawing by Goya: Spanish peasantry, equipped only with knives and sharpened stakes, fling themsleves upon French soldiers armed with muskets and bayonets.

The combat and capture of Landshut, 27 April 1809. Only Massena's unaccustomed slowness enabled Archduke John to escape. Here General Mouton leads the storming of the key bridge.

their forces split in two - around Augsburg and Ratisbon respectively - and to risk being defeated in detail. 'In this position of affairs, I greatly desire the arrival of your Majesty', wrote Berthier. His Majesty was fortunately on his way. Leaving Paris on the 13th, Napoleon reached Donauwörth on the 17th. He at once took steps to reconcentrate the whole army behind the River Ilm and near Ingolstadt, even if it meant abandoning Ratisbon.

The situation remained fraught with danger, but fortunately for the French the Austrians moved slowly. Davout was able to fight his way out of Ratisbon to link with Lefebvre's weak corps, Lannes, newly arrived from Spain, was given an extemporised command, and Massena and Oudinot made some progress from Augsburg in an attempt to arrive near the Austrian flank and rear. The confused five

The Archduke Charles brother of the Emperor Francis of Austria, was one of Napoleon's ablest opponents despite his tendency to epileptic fits. He defeated the Emperor at Aspern-Essling, 21-22 May 1808, but went down at Wagram two months later after a bitter fight.

As mortars drop bombs into the Old City, French troops swarm forward over pontoon bridges to occupy Vienna, 13 May 1809.

days of fighting came to a climax at the double battle of Abensburg-Eckmühl on 20-22 April. On the 20th, Napoleon broke through the Austrian centre, and this forced Archduke John, commanding the isolated Austrian left wing, to retreat hurriedly for Landshut on the River Isar, and only Massena's slowness on the road saved him from catastrophic defeat. Two days later, leaving a force under Bessiéres to pursue the enemy left beyond Landshut, Napoleon advanced the rest of his forces against the Austrian right-wing corps (which Davout had successfully pinned and contained), and defeated them at Eckmühl. The result of these manœuvres was the splitting of the Austrian army and its defeat in detail, but for once the French pursuit after Eckmühl was not pressed and this enabled Archduke Charles to withdraw the bulk of his forces to the north bank of the Danube through Ratisbon. But the road to Vienna now lay open before Napoleon. The situation had been transformed.

For their part, the French needed a brief chance to rest and reorganise; and it was also considered necessary to regain Ratisbon. This was accomplished by Lannes on the 23rd; Napoleon received a slight wound to his right foot during the morning, but continued in over-all command - to the relief of his men. The, leaving the experienced Davout to press Charles north of the Danube, and sending Lefebvre to watch the approaches to the Tyrol, the Emperor marched on the Austrian capital. Reinforcements were on the point of reaching him - the Imperial Guard on transfer from Spain, and Bernadotte at the head of the Saxon contingent from Dresden. The advance gained fresh impetus from news of a French setback at Sacile in north Italy: for pressure on Vienna would also distract the Austrians in Italy. On 13 May, Vienna opened its gates to the French conqueror.

By now the French battle-strength at Vienna, despite reinforcements, was only eight-two thousand. No less than ninety-four thousand troops (excluding Eugène Beauharnais's fifty-seven thousand in north Italy) were engaged on secondary duties south of the Danube - containing or besieging Austrian detachments, guarding the extensive communications and coping with a rash of local risings: even Davout's corps had been reallocated to these duties. Archduke Charles, however, had massed 115,000 men quite close to Vienna in great secrecy. Napoleon was unaware of this, but he knew that part of the Archduke John's force was marching hot-foot from Italy, and this made it all the more important to reach conclusions with Charles, once he was located.

The first requirement was to secure a bridgehead on the Danube's northern bank. The site selected was opposite the Isle of Lobau, four miles below Vienna, and the French sappers at once began to construct a bridge on to the island while a feint was mounted at Nussdorf above Vienna. The work began on 13 May. But unknown to Napoleon, Charles was moving closer to the Danube, determined to contain any French crossing, and French intelligence had failed to discover his plan.

The crossing began late on 20 May, Massena's IV Corps leading; Lobau had been occupied without opposition the previous day, and a further bridge was thrown from the island on to the Muhlau salient. Then problems arose. The Austrians upstream sent down a series of floating mills, and the first of these smashed through the vital main bridge. Only by morning could the flow of troops be resumed - but there was still no sign of the Austrian army. Charles, however, knew every French move, and at 10 am on the 21st he ordered five columns to attack along a six-mile front against Aspern, Essling and Gross-Enzersdorf. Shortly after 1 pm, the battle opened, to the amazement of the French.

Caught straddled over the river, with the rearward bridge being put repeatedly out of action, the French army was not in an

enviable position. Before the day was out, the French had managed
to pass a total of 31,400 men into the action, but the foe was three
times as strong. Thanks to superb fighting, in which both Massena
and Lannes took a major share, and to over-caution on the part of
the Austrians, the French managed to cling on to the villages. The
French heavy cavalry also shared in this achievement, narrowly
averting the danger of annihilation until nightfall brought a
welcome pause.

Once the bridges were in operation, the French were able to build
up their strength to 62,000 men and 144 guns by dawn. They were
still massively outnumbered, but Napoleon was determined to
fight. At 7 am Lannes and Oudinot attacked the centre of the
Austrian line. The Austrians recoiled, until Charles in person rallied
the line. The French began to run short of ammunition, and
Bessiére's attempts to keep the initiative with a series of cavalry
charges also failed. Worst of all, the bridge had parted again, which
meant that Davout's corps could not cross to build the French army,
now 73,000 strong, to the strength needed to win the day.

By midday the bridge was open again, but only briefly before a
new gap was torn. Napoleon now took the hard decision to call off
the battle, and withdraw his weary men on to Lobau Island. Given
the renewed pressure by the Austrians, this was not easy to achieve,
and the Young Guard (newly raised in 1809) had to be employed to
win a breathing space. At the insistence of both his officers and his
men, the Guard threatening to down arms if he stayed near the
fighting, Napoleon handed over command of the withdrawal to
Lannes. By 3.30 am on the 23rd, the last troops were on Lobau, and
the forward bridge was dismantled.

There is no disguising that Aspern-Essling had ended in a French
defeat. For the loss of 22,000 men, the French may have inflicted
23,000 casualties on the Austrians, but they had been repulsed from
the north bank. Napoleon had committed grave errors. To cross the
river, relying on a single bridge, and with no accurate knowledge of
the foe's positions, had been to court disaster. Poor reconnaissance,
lack of surprise, non-existent measures for protecting the bridge -
these factors, together with the sound plan of the Archduke
Charles, account for this serious setback. Above all, it was an ill-
planned operation; a gamble that failed to come off. Worst, Lannes
was mortally wounded.

Napoleon, however, could learn from his mistakes. While the
Austrians did nothing to exploit their success, the Emperor at once
started on new plans. Six weeks of preparation followed. Lobau

Island was converted into a fortress, mounting 129 guns. Two sturdy bridges - with up-stream break-waters and stockades to ward off floating missiles - linked Lobau with the south bank by late June; gun-boat flotillas were also stationed on the river. The army's artillery was built up to a total of 500 pieces, and massive reinforcements were summoned to the area, including Eugéne and Macdonald from the south, Marmont from Graz and Davout from Pressburg. By 1 July 160,000 troops were close to Vienna, and more were drawing near. As for the Austrians, Charles did little besides strengthening his fortifications facing Lobau; his hopes of a general German rising against the French proved illusory, and he was anxious about belated Russian manœuvres in Galicia.

In early July Napoleon moved on to Lobau, and the Muhlau salient was reoccupied to distract Austrian attention. Napoleon's plan called for a massive crossing to the east, rather than to the north, of Lobau Island across extemporised bridges, followed by a mighty wheel to take the line of villages in flank and rear. Charles meantime, aware that something was in the wind, consulted with his generals about the best measures to adopt. They eventually decided to man the villages only lightly, drawing up the main army along the northern edge of the Marchfield Plain with the centre near the village of Deutsch-Wagram and the left behind the Russbach stream. By this time, Austrian strength had grown to almost 155,000.

During the stormy night of 4 July, the French plan was put into operation, just as the last formations were hurried on to Lobau Island. Eight pontoon bridges were suddenly swung from the east side of the island, and troops led by Massena's IV Corps began to pour on to the north bank of the Danube. The crossing went like clockwork with minimal confusion. All bridges held, and the local enemy troops were overwhelmed, though the main Austrian forces were not encountered at first.

The capture of Gross-Enzersdorf by mid-morning enabled a new bridge to be built, and provided the French army with a useful pivot for deploying for the main battle. By mid-afternoon the French, at Napoleon's order, set about enlarging their bridgehead; Aspern and Essling were both captured. By 5 pm, Massena was in position on the far left facing the Bissamberg near Florisdorf, and the front line was completed by Bernadotte's IX Corps, Eugéne's 'Army of Italy', Oudinot's II Corps and, on the extreme right, Davout's III Corps, with the Guard and Cavalry Reserve in central support, not to forget a single division and 8,000 cavalry on the

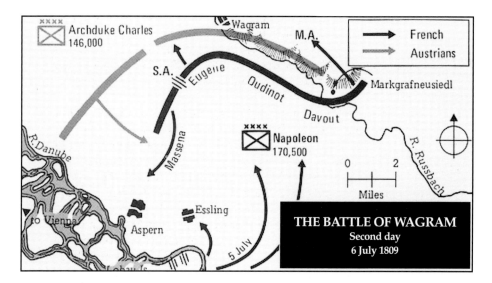

extreme right watching for any signs of the arrival of Archduke
John's 12,500 men from Pressburg. In all, Napoleon now had
136,000 in the field, and a further 17,000 were close to the bridges.

Hoping to snatch a quick victory that evening, Napoleon ordered
his right and centre to attack the enemy positioned behind the
Russbach. Unfortunately, some of Eugéne's troops were routed and
Oudinot checked, and these set-backs meant that the battle would
have to be renewed the following day. Archduke Charles, cheered
by the evening's events, was soon planning an attempt to surprise
and roll-up the French left wing, from the direction of the
Bissamberg, and thus cut off the French from Lobau. Napoleon, too,
was issuing his orders. Massena on the left was to be on the
defensive; the centre was to distract the Austrians with local
attacks; the main move was to be by Davout on the right, with the
Army of Italy ready to launch the breakthrough attempt in the
centre when the moment came.

The Austrians got in the first blow on the 6th, by a secondary
attack against Davout. No sooner had this been checked, and
Davout told to implement the main plan, than news came that
Bernadotte's Saxons were routed near Aderklaa. Napoleon
forthwith dismissed the Marshal from his command. Then, at about
8 am, came the main Austrian onslaught against one of Massena's
divisions. Some 37,000 men came out of the mist, and soon
Massena's 8,000 were in full retreat. Fortunately, Eugène
extemporised a linking line with Macdonald's troops and corps

artillery. Then Napoleon arrived to take charge. He cunningly moved Massena's remaining troops southwards behind the firing line, brought the left back to the level of Lobau Island so that its massed guns could be brought to bear and filled the gap thus caused in his centre by deploying the artillery reserve in a vast battery of 122 guns.

These measures served to stabilise the situation on his left. It still remained to win the day. Shortly after midday, Davout's slow but steady attack had pressed back the Austrian left through Markgrafneusiedl. At this moment, the French battle-line was shaped like an immense 'Z'. The time had come for the *coup de grâce,* and Eugène's Army of Italy swept forward. It failed to break through, but the Archduke Charles had seen enough. Despairing of his brother's appearance from Pressburg, he ordered a general retreat, but it was not until the 7th that Napoleon realised that all was over. For 32,000 casualties, the French had inflicted forty thousand on the Austrians.

There was no immediate pursuit, but the Austrians were demoralised, and after four days of manœuvres, an armistice was signed. Later, after several months of wrangling, the Peace of Pressburg was signed on 14 October. Three million Austrian subjects incorporated in boundary adjustments, a huge indemnity and a restricted army were the price of failure. Napoleon had again been the victor, but by only a narrow margin.

Austria's defeat in the Wagram campaign seemed to have re-established Napoleon's authority in Europe more conclusively and dazzlingly than ever. But appearances were deceptive, and his very success held within it the seeds of ultimate failure. For, in the last resort, it was impossible for one nation to subdue an entire continent. The fervour of Revolution, and the revolutionary ideals which Napoleon claimed to represent, indeed gave his armies a spirit and cohesion unmatched by those of the backward, antiquated regimes he had confronted. Yet the disasters he inflicted did not eliminate those regimes; rather they forced them to have to re-think, to modernise and to become potentially ever more formidable. Moreover, Napoleon's victories were not followed by the reforms hoped for by his liberal admirers. Liberals and nationalists in Germany and elsewhere, who had once prayed for his success, now looked to his downfall as the only way to relieve Europe of military oppression. Plots against his life became more frequent, not only from right-wing extremists but now from left-wing patriots. Increasingly he was opposed by Europe's peoples as

Napoleon's early passion of 1796 turned somewhat sour in 1798 when he learned of Josephine's marital indiscretions but, aware that his own record was not in this respect 'sans réproche', he resisted all attempts by his family to force a divorce. However, her continuing infertility became increasingly awkward, and the Emperor was feeling that the establishment of a dynasty must take precedence over all other issues and considerations. So he chose the Austrian Archduchess Marie-Louise to be his second wife. The Empress Josephine pleaded with Napoleon to reconsider his decision. He remained adamant. However, on his deathbed at St Helena, her name was one of the last words he uttered.

well as by their governments. For himself, Napoleon had set a course on which there was no going back. The Continent would not accept his hegemony by agreement; he would be compelled to continue from one campaign to the next to achieve stability by force against ever more potent enemies, prepared to forget their own dissensions in the face of the threat he posed. Moreover, at this stage in his career, the Emperor was no longer the man he had once been. Some physical deteriorations had begun. His mental powers were not quite so pronounced and he was beginning to suffer that fate of all conquerors - a dangerous belief in his own infallibity.

It was at this critical juncture that Napoleon made a change in his personal life. He had long been alarmed by Josephine's failure to produce an heir, and now the possibility of assassination made him determined to safeguard the dynasty at the expense of his wife. Accordingly, despite Josephine's frantic remonstrations and his own genuine fondness of her, she was divorced; and, in February 1810, he was betrothed to Marie-Louise, daughter of the Austrian Emperor.

Marie-Louise displays the King of Rome.

It was a marriage which brought personal happiness and, on 20 March 1811, the longed-for son, who was christened Francis Charles Joseph and promptly proclaimed King of Rome. But the

Napoleon was delighted with his son and on the eve of Borodino proudly displayed for his troops a new portrait.

marriage meant something else, for it symbolised a growing rift with Russia whose government had also been negotiating for a marital alliance with the Emperor. The collapse of these negotiations did not cause, but certainly underlined, the breakdown of the spirit of Tilsit.

The breach with Russia had been complex and gradual. The aftermath of Erfurt was one source of strain, but it was soon eclipsed by others. From the Tsar's viewpoint, there were several bones of contention. There was the unpopularity of the Continental System in high Court circles, and the presence of French troops east of the River Oder which was deeply resented, for Russia had always regarded Poland as its front-yard. Thirdly, Russian statesmen challenged Napoleon's determination to restrict Russian expansion in the Balkan region at the expense of the Turks; and finally, of course, the Tsar could not but regard Napoleon's abrupt marriage to an Austrian princess as a deliberate affront to the Romanov family honour.

Napoleon, too, had his grievances. He could not tolerate Russia's bare-faced flouting of his economic sanctions against Britain. Russian intrusions into the affairs of the grand duchy of Warsaw and continued probes towards Constantinople appeared to reveal dark secret ambitions totally contrary to French interests. The Russian Minister of War, Barclay de Tolly, was also known to be hurrying through a modernisation of the Russian army along French lines - another portent of trouble.

By late 1811 both sides were preparing for war. Russian engineers fortified the Dvina-Dnieper river-lines, while Napoleon built up depots in Prussia and Poland and began creating a vast army in eastern Europe, bullying a dozen countries into providing contingents. Uniquely, he also organised twenty-six transport battalions with which to supply them, for he was aware that western Russia would present grave logistical problems due to its underdeveloped condition.

In May 1812 the French had massed all of 650,000 troops. It might be thought that the threat alone would have brought the Tsar to seek a *rapprochement*; that it did not, equally indicated that the Russians would offer a determined opposition. Nevertheless, Napoleon prophesied a quick, victorious campaign of some five weeks' duration. At this stage, he had no intention whatsoever of marching to Moscow to dictate a victor's peace. A two-week conference with his confederates, both willing and unwilling, including the Emperor Francis and the King of Prussia, was held at

Dresden in an attempt to bring Alexander to his senses. However, in the diplomatic offensive preceding the outbreak of war, the Tsar indubitably came off best. Sweden professed friendly neutrality; accommodations were patched up on the Finnish and Moldavian fronts, thus releasing Russian armies, and in July Great Britain would promise money and the presence of a fleet in the Baltic. On the other hand, pending the transfer of forces from the peripheral areas, Russia could immediately field only some 220,000 men, in two armies, in the west by mid-June, under the command of Barclay de Tolly and Bagration, based upon the command of Vilna and Volkovisk, respectively. A third army under Tormassov was in process of formation far to the south.

As Alexander would not retreat, Napoleon was ready to strike. *La Grande Armée de Russie* was organised into a central group of three armies, commanded by Napoleon, Eugène and Jerome respectively, echeloned back to Warsaw, with semi-autonomous corps on each distant flank. Behind these 449,000 troops, two lines of reserve formations stretched back into central Germany. However, owing to the operations in Spain, which were tying down over two hundred thousand French troops, less than half Napoleon's vast array was composed of French nationals. Thus its reliability was uncertain, in both military and political terms; and problems of command, language, supply and control would prove daunting when added to those of distance. Napoleon's plan, however, envisaged a quick victory. He selected the region north of the Pripet marshes for his offensive - it was nearer to his main bases at Danzig and Königsberg, posed a double threat (towards Moscow or St Petersburg) and would permit a closer supervision of unreliable Prussia. From there, he planned to cross the River Nieman near Kovno with his main force, supported by Eugéne's army, in order to break through Barclay's extended forces and destroy them piecemeal by use of envelopment attacks. Meanwhile, Jerome's army was to lure Bagration towards Warsaw prior to pinning him at the River Narew or Bug, while part of the northern French forces, having dealt with Barclay, swept into his rear. The flanking corps, commanded by Macdonald and the Austrian Schwarzenberg respectively, were to keep abreast with the major formations, pressing up the Baltic coastline towards Riga or deep into Volhynia. As for the Russians, their strategy would seem to have envisaged a withdrawal towards the fortified river-lines before making a determined stand to hold the 'river gap', while Bagration attacked the French flank from the south.

On 24 June, after closing up to the Niemen and establishing a
number of bridges, the *Grande Armée poured* forward into Russian
Poland. From the first, however, its advance was hampered by the
unaccustomed reliance on slow-moving transport and food
columns. As a result, and also due to Russian elusiveness, a
succession of separate attempts failed to trap the enemy into a
decisive engagement. The first, the manœuvre of Vilna, 24 June-8
July, saw Murat's successful capture of Barclay's former
headquarters, but Napoleon's corps were unable to exploit this
owing to Eugène's inability to move up in support of their right
flank. Farther south, Jérôme proved wholly incapable of either
luring or pinning Bagration, who set out almost at once for the
north-east hoping to join Barclay. As a result, when Davout led a
rapid lunge southwards from Vilna, he struck empty air. Stung by
Napoleon's criticisms, Jerome promptly abandoned his command
and left the front for Westphalia.

After a brief pause to reorganise his scattered formations, and to
bring his chaotic rear areas into some form of order, Napoleon
transferred his full attention to the northern sector, and made a
second attempt to trap Barclay on the Dvina near the fortified
positions of Dunaburg and Drissa, while Davout, in temporary
command of Jerome's army, pursued Bagration with orders to
prevent a link-up by the Russian forces at all costs. The operations
between 16 and 26 July again failed to force a battle, but the
Russians were compelled to abandon their defensive river-line
barrier. Up to this time, the Russian retreat was probably deliberate,
but now the only strategy open to them was dictated by the need to
survive, and the hope that they could join their two armies together.
In fact, Bagration's 48,000 men were steadily converging with
Barclay's 110,000, despite repeated French efforts to interpose a
force between them. Napoleon's chances of defeating a divided foe
in detail were fast diminishing, and he had already been drawn
farther into Russia than he had originally anticipated.

Another pause followed, but then, between 22 and 26 August, the
French advanced once more, this time towards Smolensk. The
blazing heat of summer was taking its toll of men and horses alike,
and far away in Volhynia the newly-formed Russian Third Army
was in action against both Reynier's VII Corps and Schwarzenberg.
Severe fighting was also reported by Oudinot around Pulotsk to the
north. By this time, the French front already measured all of five
hundred miles, and problems of control were fast becoming
insuperable. Even worse, on 4 August, Barclay and Bagration had at

Prince Golenischev-Kutusov, Russian commander-in-chief at Borodino and for the remainder of the campaign of 1812. Although already an old man, Kutusov knew how to inspire the peasant-soldiers of Russia.

last linked up to the west of Smolensk, though the two generals were soon in bitter disagreement.

Seeking to retrieve the situation, Napoleon hurled his main forces into the 'river gap.' Using Murat to draw the Russians westwards towards Inkovo on 8 August, the bulk of the army crossed the Dnieper in a surprise move and attempted to sweep on to Smolensk, there to sever the Russian line of retreat to the east. Thanks to the stalwart fighting by a single Russian corps south of the Dnieper, however, the French advance was slowed, and this gave Barclay and Bagration time to realise their danger and, on the 15th, to order a pell-mell retreat to Smolensk and to forestall the French. For three days, 17-19 August, a serious battle raged around Smolensk's southern outskirts, but the result was an indecisive French victory. For a cost of 10,000 casualties, the French inflicted perhaps 12,000 on their enemy, but, thanks to General Junot's failure to cut the vital Smolensk-Moscow highway near Lubino to the east of the city, the Russians were again able to retreat in fighting order. Yet another attempt to force a decisive battle had come to nothing.

So far, great inroads had been made into Russian territory, but there were no signs of a weakening Russian resolve, and already the French rear was under spasmodic attack by Cossacks and partisans. The Emperor now faced the critical decision of the campaign. Should he press on, or hold his position for the winter before mounting a new effort in 1813?

In the end, Napoleon's instinct as a gambler forced him on, even though his front now extended for all of seven hundred miles from flank to flank, and the battle power of his central army group had dwindled to only 156,000 men. Moscow still lay 280 miles ahead, but rather than lose it, Napoleon argued, the Russians would surely accept a decisive battle. So the advance was resumed from 28 August. The fatal decision had been taken.

By this time, the Tsar had become increasingly critical of his commanders' conduct of the campaign, and from 20 August the highest command was entrusted to Kutusov, now a veteran of sixty-seven, with direct orders to fight for Moscow, the capital and Holy City of Russia. He selected a position some seventy miles west of Moscow, and prepared for battle near the township of Borodino. On 5 September the leading elements of the French arrived from the west, and captured the out-lying Schivardino Redoubt.

The 6th passed in probes and reconnaissances, as both sides completed their preparations. The Emperor was unwell, his spirits not being improved by the arrival of news of Marmont's defeat at Salamanca in far-away Spain. However, the arrival of a portrait of the King of Rome was a welcome interlude. As the day progressed, Napoleon drew up his plan. Rejecting Davout's plea for an outflanking sweep to the south, he settled for a massive

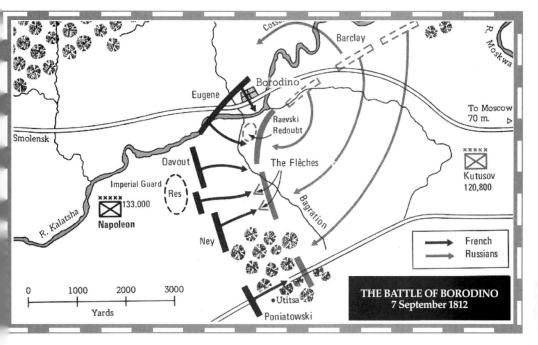

THE BATTLE OF BORODINO
7 September 1812

Smolensk · R. Kalatsha · Eugene · Borodino · Davout · Imperial Guard · Res · Napoleon 133,000 · Ney · Raevski Redoubt · The Flèches · Bagration · Utitsa · Poniatowski · Barclay · Cossa... · R. Moskwa · To Moscow 70 m. · Kutusov 120,800

French
Russians

0 1000 2000 3000
Yards

bombardment, a clearing action against Borodino on the left, a tactical outflanking attack on the far right near Utitsa and a main attack against the centre of the Russian position, which was guarded by the *flèches* earthworks and the imposing Raevski Redoubt. Kutusov, for his part, placed almost half of his 120,800 men and 680 cannon behind the Kalatsha river on his right, in the belief that Napoleon would try to outflank that wing.

On the 7th, the battle began as the 133,000 French, aided by 585 cannon, began to advance. On the left, Eugène rapidly cleared Borodino, but on the right, Poniatowski was soon held up in the woodland around Utitsa. In the centre, a massive battle of attrition raged, as three French corps were sent progressively into action. The fortunes of war swung to and fro over the critical fieldworks, but nowhere could the French establish a true mastery. Shortly after midday, Kutusov launched five thousand cavalry and Cossacks against the French in Borodino, and Napoleon had to return troops to contain the danger. This earned the Russians a respite, during which Kutusov redeployed his right-wing corps in support of his centre.

Prince Poniatowski, Polish patriot and soldier. An able soldier, he was drowned at Leipzig on 19 October, 1813, only a few hours after being awarded his marshal's baton.

Napoleon played a negative role in the day's events. When, following a renewed all-out onslaught supported by 400 guns, the Raevski Redoubt at last passed into French hands and the chance of victory seemed real, he repeatedly refused to send in his last reserve - namely the Guard. The Russians were therefore given the chance to withdraw to a neighbouring ridge, where they again turned defiantly. By dusk, a lull born of mutual exhaustion settled over the terrible scene, which held thirty thousand French and perhaps forty-four thousand Russian casualties. The French expected the battle to be renewed the next day, but Kutusov, against the advice of his generals, determined to withdraw overnight with his 90,000 battle-worthy survivors.

The prize of this incomplete French victory was Moscow, occupied on 14 September. But Napoleon found the city almost deserted, and a day later a great fire laid two-thirds of Moscow in smouldering ruins. Kutusov's army - still in being - drew off to the south-east of the capital, biding time. Alexander still refused to countenance French peace proposals, and over a period of weeks it gradually became apparent to Napoleon that he had entirely misinterpreted both the Tsar's character and his people's indomitable will to resist. His situation grew steadily more critical. With only 95,000 operational troops left, the French were soon outnumbered even by Kutusov, now reinforced to 110,000. Worse, fresh Russian armies were approaching - Steinheil and Wittgenstein from Finland, and Tshitsagov from Moldavia - and the strategic initiative was passing to his opponents. The Emperor was also aware of two other detrimental factors - the depradations being carried out against his over-extended communications by Russian irregulars, and the steady approach of winter. Then, on the 18th, Murat's cavalry was severely shaken by a Russian surprise attack south-east of Moscow. By then Napoleon had already decided to retreat. So it was that on the 120th day of the campaign, the French quitted Moscow, much impeded by the loot of the capital.

The battle of Borodino, although indecisive, opened the road to Moscow for the French, and they duly occupied a near-deserted city a week later. News about Borodino's outcome was confused, and General Wilson (not present at the battle) reported to Lord Castlereagh that the French had been defeated. The day after the French occupation, however, a major fire devastated two-thirds of the city, only the Kremlin quarter surviving relatively unscathed. Whether this was the work of Russian incendiaries (as seems probable) or of looting Frenchman, remains a subject for debate. After several weeks hoping that Alexander would sue for peace, Napoleon ordered the retreat. At first all went reasonably well, but as he approached Smolensk the first heavy snow-storms and severe frosts began.

One of the few figures to gain repute from this period was Michel Ney, Marshal and Duke of Elchingen. His gallant conduct of the rearguard earned him the sobriquet of 'the bravest of the brave'. More renowned for his courage than his brains, Ney was eventually executed by the Bourbons in December 1815.

The tide had turned.

Napoleon's first plan was to retire on Smolensk through the prosperous and unravaged countryside around Kaluga to the south. But between 23 and 25 October, a sharp brush with part of Kutusov's army at Malo-Jaroslavetz - in which the Emperor was almost taken captive - persuaded him to swing his march back to the original line of advance. The fifty-mile-long French column found its retreat over the already twice-ravaged countryside continually harassed by Cossacks and partisans, though Kutusov held off, moving parallel and to the south of the French. Soon French supply arrangements broke down, and the cohesion of the once *Grande Armée* began to crack. Smolensk and its considerable depots were reached on and after 9 November, but the famished and indisciplined soldiery destroyed most of the stores in a burst of wanton destruction. By this time, the first snows and frosts had been encountered, and Russian attacks were increasing, resulting in the separation of Ney and the rearguard from the main body - although he would subsequently rejoin after an epic march.

Napoleon could not linger at Smolensk. He was already aware that he was engaged in a race against time, for new Russian armies were converging from the north and south, driving in the over-extended French flanks into a narrowing corridor. The danger was that these forces would get ahead of the French and sever their line of retreat towards Poland. On the 12th, therefore, the head of the French column left Smolensk and five days later Napoleon

Soon the army's cohesion began to break down and the retreat became a rout.

launched the Guard in a telling attack against a Russian force at Krasnöe. This determined Kutusov not to press for a major engagement. The French situation was, this notwithstanding, becoming increasingly desperate. On the 18th alarming news arrived that Tshitsagov had captured the crucial French depots at Minsk. Then everyone's spirits were raised by the near-miraculous reappearance of Ney, whom Napoleon promptly dubbed 'the bravest of the brave'. His valiant fighting and marching enabled him to save 900 men of his corps. By this juncture, there were barely 40,000 French soldiers combat-worthy, with a rabble of perhaps twice as many stragglers, clinging to the rear of the column.

On 22 October dire news arrived from the town of Borisov, revealing that Tshitsagov at the head of 30,000 men had indeed won the race to the River Beresina, and destroyed the vital bridges ahead of the French. Napoleon ordered that his state papers be destroyed, and prepared for the worst. An unseasonable thaw had turned the Beresina into a torrent, and there seemed little chance of his army surviving as Wittgenstein, thirty thousand strong, closed in from the north, pushing Victor's and Oudinot's depleted corps before him, and Kutusov, very warily, moved up from the rear with 65,000 more. It seemed that the trap must close about Napoleon.

A combination of luck and brilliant generalship saved Napoleon and his eagles. With great skill, he succeeded in fooling Tshitsagov, and thanks to the selfless exertions of his pontoon train, two bridges were built across the Beresina near Studienka at a fortunately discovered ford. Between 25 and 29 November the French poured over the river, while desperate fighting broke out along both banks. Nevertheless, the Russians had spoiled their opportunity, and possibly 40,000 French survivors escaped the trap before the bridges were destroyed - but some 50,000 dead or captured, many of them non-combatants, had been the price.

The road to Vilna and Poland now lay open before the emaciated French forces. Napoleon left the army to its despair on 5 December, to return to Paris, there to quash rumours of his death which had already resulted in one near-successful conspiracy, and to start building new armies. Commanded by a disgruntled Murat, the survivors staggered on towards Poland, encountering terrible weather conditions which added still further to the loss of life. The King of Naples soon departed in his turn for his sunny kingdom, and it was left to Eugène to supervise the last stages of the retreat. The Russians were now content to leave the French to the weather and made no further serious attempts to come to grips. So it was, therefore, that the New Year of 1813 saw some 94,000 French and Allied survivors (to include the flanking forces which suffered less drastically, though General Yorck led some twenty thousand Prussians into the Russian camp on 3 December) come out of Russia; by this time, the 400,000 men of the original central army group was reduced to 25,000.

The legend of French invincibility now lay utterly shattered. But the Russians had lost at least 125,000 soldiers and perhaps a million civilians since June 1812. However, the soil of Holy Russia was clear of the invader, and preparations for the liberation of Germany were soon being put in hand as Prussia - ever resentful of the French yoke - approved General Yorck's action on 13 March and prepared to defect.

CHAPTER FIVE

Defeat and Abdication
1813-15

Terrible as were the disasters of 1812, few could have foreseen that the following year would see Napoleon's Empire disintegrate. But, for the Emperor, time was running out. In February 1813, Prussia signed an alliance with Russia, and it remained only for Austria to take the field once more and all Europe would be in arms against him. Napoleon could scarcely believe that Austria, now tied dynastically to France, would mobilise against him; but her Foreign Minister, Metternich, was prepared to consider a settlement only if France abandoned her German conquests and suppressed the grand duchy of Warsaw and the Confederation of the Rhine. For Napoleon, such a diplomatic defeat was unthinkable. As he told Metternich, 'Your Sovereigns born on the throne can let themselves be beaten twenty times and return to their capitals. I cannot do this because I am an important soldier. My domination will not survive the day when I cease to be strong and therefore feared.'

The campaign of France, 1814. The sands were running out for Napoleon as massive allied armies invaded the soil of France, but he still managed a virtuoso performance with the scanty resources available.

In the end, Napoleon's inability to reverse the course he had set himself would mean his destruction. For the moment, his immediate task was to repair as far as possible the damage of the Russian campaign and prepare to face his Russian and Prussian enemies in the field. Back in Paris, he found that 137,000 conscripts were completing their initial training. To these he added eighty thousand men embodied from the National Guard, called up a proportion of the conscript class of 1814 and a further hundred thousand from the classes of 1808 and 1809-10, transferred 12,000 from the navy and 3,000 from the gendarmerie, demanded 20,000 from the French municipalities and 30,000 from Italy. France became one vast workshop, as superhuman efforts were called for to clothe and equip these new forces. The gravest problem was the shortage of horses, and hence the deficiency of cavalry, while in terms of quality the new levies left very much to be desired. Yet somehow, despite the continued drain of the Spanish front, where Wellington was rapidly establishing the upper hand, another half million men were found for the battles to be fought in Germany.

A German cartoon of 1813 represents Napoleon's tyrannical hold on Germany. The word 'Arps' on the epaulette is the name of a patriotic German printer executed by the French. The 'uniform' comprises a map showing the battles fought in 1813 during the war of German liberation.

Napoleon had ordered Eugène to fall back to the River Elbe near Magdeburg, there to cover the formation of the new French army near Mainz as Kutusov advanced over the Oder with a first wave of 120,000 men, spread over a broad front. By mid-April Napoleon had assembled 226,000 men and 457 guns. His first plan envisaged a savage advance through Prussia to relieve besieged Danzig, but his strength was not yet sufficient for this task, especially as the Confederation of the Rhine was restive, and Dresden threatened. Accordingly, on 29 March, he decided to advance from Erfurt on Leipzig in the hope of snatching a quick victory and compelling the

Allies to retire back over the Elbe. Thereafter, he hoped to march on Berlin. But from the start, the French were hampered by insufficient information of the foe's exact whereabouts: their shortage of cavalry gravely affected their operational efficiency throughout 1813.

By 25 April the Emperor was at Erfurt, and while the Army of the Elbe under Eugéne advanced through Merseburg to distract the foe, the Army of the Main swept towards Lutzen. There, on 2 May, the Emperor won the battle of Lutzen against General Wittgenstein. The action was unexpected by the French (due to weak reconnaissance), but Napoleon jumped at the chance, and thanks to the superb mobility of his corps was able to increase his fighting force in the area from an initial 45,000 to 110,000, which was more than enough to defeat the 75,000 Prussians and Russians. The enemy, however, were able to retire on Bautzen relatively unharassed, for once again French shortage of cavalry precluded an all-out pursuit. Nevertheless, the Emperor ordered a general

The battle of Lutzen, 2 May 1813. Napoleon proved incapable of exploiting this success owing to lack of cavalry.

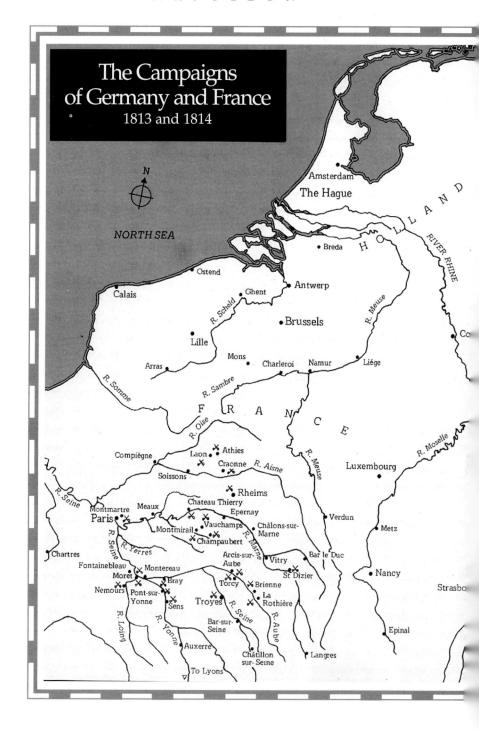

The Campaigns of Germany and France
1813 and 1814

N

NORTH SEA

Amsterdam
The Hague

HOLLAND

RIVER RHINE

• Breda

Ostend
Calais
• Ghent
Antwerp

R. Scheld
R. Meuse

• Brussels

Lille
•

Mons
•
Charleroi
Namur
Liége

Arras •
R. Sambre

R. Somme

F R A N C E

R. Oise

R. Moselle

Compiègne
Laon • ✕ Athies
✕ Craonne
R. Aisne
R. Meuse
Luxembourg
•

Soissons

✕ Rheims

R. Seine
Montmartre
Meaux
Chateau Thierry
Epernay
Verdun
•

Paris ✕
✕ ✕ Vauchamps
Châlons-sur-Marne
Metz
•

✕ Montmirail
R. Marne

Champaubert

• Chartres
R. Seine
R. Yerres
Arcis-sur-Aube
✕ Vitry
Bar le Duc
Nancy
•

Fontainebleau
✕ Montereau
✕ Torcy
St Dizier

Moret ✕ Bray
✕ Brienne
Nemours Pont-sur-Yonne
Sens
Troyes
La Rothière
Strasbo

R. Loing
R. Yonne
Bar-sur-Seine
R. Seine
R. Aube
Epinal
•

Auxerre •
Châtillon sur-Seine
• Langres

To Lyons

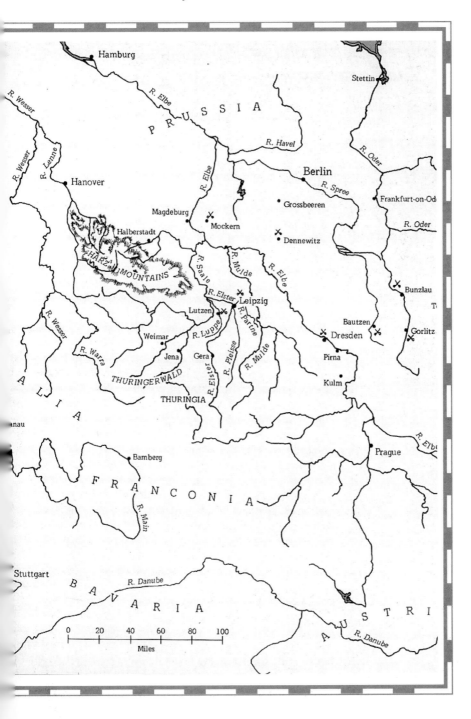

advance on Bautzen, where Wittgenstein, now reinforced to 96,000 strong, had taken up a strong position behind the River Spree. Typically, Napoleon decided to attack as soon as possible. Rapidly reorganising the two French armies into a single force, Napoleon advanced with 115,000 men to mount a frontal attack while Ney, entrusted with 84,000 troops, swept down from the north in a classical envelopment. On 20 May Napoleon fought alone, pinning the enemy to the area, and next day Ney arrived in strength. The Allies were defeated, though the French failed to mount an effective pursuit; the plan had been excellent, but the execution faulty and the result was, therefore, inconclusive.

Both sides needed a breathing space, and on 2 June agreed to an armistice. The negotiations which followed were neither successful nor wholly sincere, but served to win time while armies were strengthened and diplomats talked. By the end of the summer, when fighting was renewed, it was evident that the French had been out-manœuvred. Austria had at last joined the Allies, and the Crown Prince of Sweden, Bernadotte, Napoleon's former Marshal, had done the same. The Allies now had an overall preponderance of man-power, perhaps 800,000 to his total of 700,000, the great bulk of whom were inexperienced conscripts.

Napoleon decided to make Dresden his defensive centre of operation, massing his stores there and deploying his forces between the Oder and the Elbe to make the most of his central position. By mid-August he had some three hundred thousand troops in the region; opposing him was an army under Bernadotte, 120,000 strong, near Berlin; Blücher's Army of Silesia, 95,000 strong, around Breslau; and Schwarzenberg's 240,000 Austrians centred on Kulm to the south.

The position was desperate for the French as Napoleon sought to ward off the numerous threats facing him. His task was made no easier by the new Allied strategy of avoiding battle with the Emperor himself, but concentrating on his subordinates. Time and time again, Napoleon was forced to adjust his plans as new crises arose. On 24 August, instead of attacking Blücher as first intended, he decided to concentrate on a sweep against the rear of Schwarzenberg's Army of Bohemia through Pirna. This move was half-implemented when news arrived from the north that Oudinot was in difficulties; shortly after, he learned that St Cyr, at Dresden, was on the point of losing the vital bases to Schwarzenberg. This could not be countenanced, and the Emperor again dropped his Pirna plan in favour of a desperate rush to bolster St Cyr. The result was the battle of Dresden, 26-7 August. Napoleon arrived in time to lead seventy thousand men in repulsing the belated Allied attacks on the city; too late, the Allies realised that they were facing Napoleon in person. By the 27th Napoleon had assembled 120,000 men to face Schwarzenberg's 170,000, and with a mighty attack the French destroyed the Allied left wing. After losing 38,000 casualties to the French 10,000, Schwarzenberg ordered a retreat. Once again, however, Napoleon could not pursue effectively, and as a result the Allies were able to wipe out a force of 20,000 French isolated at Kulm, on the 29th. The previous day, Marshal Macdonald had been severely mauled by Blücher at the River Katzbach, and details of Oudinot's defeat at Grössbeeren also arrived. Thus the French success at Dresden was largely off-set by three disasters elsewhere. The omens were not propitious for the French, and the confidence and determination of the Allies increased.

Vainly Napoleon tried to organise a great drive on Berlin; instead he was forced to move to rally Macdonald's demoralised forces, and then to sweep back to Kulm to head off a renewed Austrian advance on Dresden. Worse, on 6 September Ney was repulsed at Dennewitz in the north, and soon Napoleon was again required to intervene near Dresden, and on Macdonald's sector in turn. The Allied strategy was therefore paying off: Napoleon was afforded no chance to launch a major blow; he was being played like a bull in the arena, and his overmarched troops were dropping with fatigue. Meanwhile, French influence in Germany was steadily eroding, only Saxony remaining fully loyal to Napoleon. The Emperor was forced by these developments to abandon all thought of operations east of the Elbe.

The Allies were now scenting the kill. Blücher's army was sent north to join Bernadotte as Bennigsen approached with 60,000 fresh Russians to strengthen Schwarzenberg. They also decided to concentrate all moves towards Leipzig so as to place the French links with the Rhine in jeopardy. By early October the ring was closing, and the French were driven back step by step towards Leipzig. Napoleon was still obsessed with the need to conserve Dresden, and this led him to divide his forces - a fatal step as events were to prove. With 150,000 men, Napoleon advanced north to try to envelop Blücher and Bernadotte on the River Mulde. But the Allies now knew the counter to this well-tried Napoleonic manœuvre, and refused to be flustered. On 12 October he realised that his bluff had been called, and retired on Leipzig, where Murat and Marmont were giving ground before Schwarzenberg. By the

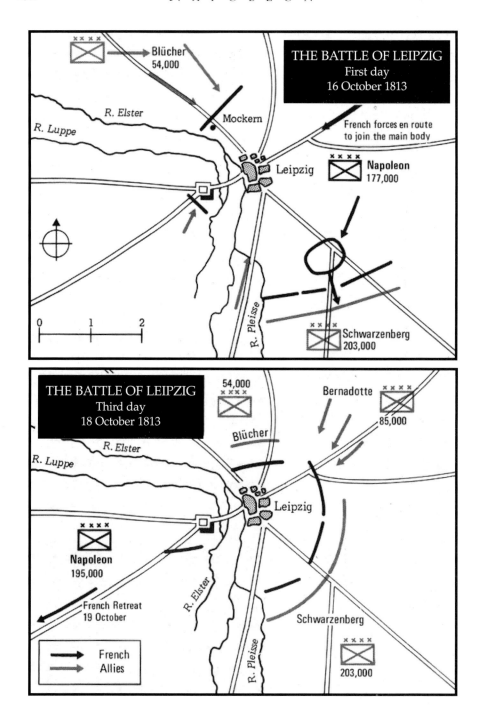

THE BATTLE OF LEIPZIG
First day
16 October 1813

Blücher
54,000

R. Elster

R. Luppe

Mockern

French forces en route
to join the main body

Leipzig

Napoleon
177,000

R. Pleisse

0   1   2

Schwarzenberg
203,000

THE BATTLE OF LEIPZIG
Third day
18 October 1813

54,000

Bernadotte

85,000

Blücher

R. Elster

R. Luppe

Leipzig

Napoleon
195,000

R. Elster

French Retreat
19 October

Schwarzenberg

R. Pleisse

203,000

French
Allies

14th Napoleon had assembled almost two hundred thousand men to face Schwarzenberg's 203,000, Blücher's converging 54,000 and Bernadotte's more distant 85,000. The climactic 'Battle of the Nations' was about to begin.

Early on the 16th, the enemy was present in strength only to the south, so Napoleon left weak forces to the north and east of the city and strained every nerve to win a victory over Schwarzenberg. But the Army of Bohemia survived the ordeal unbroken, due largely to the distraction caused by the arrival of Blücher from the north. This forced a redeployment of French forces near Mockern, where some Württemberg troops chose this moment to defect. His failure to win on the first day was fatal for Napoleon, as Allied predominance would steadily mount thereafter, to a total of 300,000 men and 1,500 guns. Napoleon would be outnumbered three to two in terms of both troops and artillery. The odds were growing long.

The 17th passed relatively quietly, as the Allies, with both Bernadotte and Bennigsen arriving, planned six concentric attacks for the 18th, with the main effort from the east. Napoleon, for his

Meeting of the Allied sovereigns at Prague, 1813 - King Frederick William III, Emperor Francis II and Tsar Alexander I.

part, planned to reduce his perimeter, and prepared for a retreat over the Rivers Elster and Luppe to the west of the city. The third day of the battle, however, saw the French line capable of holding all attacks, though some Saxon troops defected in their turn. By dusk, Napoleon was issuing orders for a general retreat. He had lost the battle.

All night the withdrawal continued, and also into the 19th. Unfortunately, the main bridge was demolished prematurely, and the French rearguard was forced to surrender. The French had lost, overall, 38,000 casualties and now 30,000 prisoners. The Allies lost at least 54,000 killed and wounded - but they had completed the liberation of Germany. Napoleon was about to be driven back west of the Rhine for ever.

For the second year running, Napoleon had lost casualties in excess of 400,000 men, and the successful retreat to the Rhine - which included a small victory at Hanau against his new Bavarian foes on 30 October - could not disguise the new, huge set-back. The reason lay partly in the inferior quality of his extemporised forces, the growing weariness of the Marshals and the increasing skill of their opponents. Napoleon had fought with skill, but his methods were now predictable, and his opponents had by now absorbed the lessons of thirteen years of Napoleonic warfare. Above all, both Napoleon and France were tiring; they had lost the initiative. It only remained for the Allies to penetrate the Empire's last stronghold, France itself.

Napoleon's defence of France is often regarded as his supreme moment. However true this may be of its technical aspects, and however much one may admire his *Götterdämmerung* performance, Napoleon must stand charged with pressing matters beyond the logical limit. In 1814, neither the people nor his commanders were wholly behind him. Delusion and egocentricity had made sad inroads on one of the greatest intellects of all time: Napoleon refused to accept the hopelessness of his position.

Somehow, between November 1813 and January 1814, Napoleon scraped together another army. Over 100,000 men were tied down in besieged fortresses beyond the Rhine, and Wellington was pinning as many more in the south of France. By dint of conscripting pensioners and mere boys, *les Marie-Louises,* a force of almost 120,000 was found for the eastern frontiers, now threatened by at least 350,000 Allies fresh from their liberation of Germany. Allied dissensions won the French a little time, but in the New Year of 1814 General Bülow advanced into Holland; Blücher crossed the

COPY

OF THE

Transparency

EXHIBITED AT

ACKERMANN'S REPOSITORY OF ARTS,

During the Illuminations of the 5th and 6th of November, 1813,

IN HONOUR OF THE SPLENDID VICTORIES OBTAINED BY

The ALLIES over the ARMIES of FRANCE,

AT LEIPSIC AND ITS ENVIRONS.

THE TWO KINGS OF TERROR.

THIS Subject, representing the two Tyrants, viz. the Tyrant BONAPARTE and the Tyrant DEATH, sitting together on the Field of Battle, in a manner which promises a more perfect intimacy immediately to ensue, is very entertaining. It is also very instructing to observe, that the former is now placed in a situation in which all Europe *may see through him*. The emblem, too, of the Circle of dazzling light from mere *vapour*, which is so *soon extinguished*, has a good moral effect; and as the Gas represents the dying flame, so does the Drum, on which he is seated, typify the *hollow* and *noisy* nature of the falling Usurper.

The above description of the subject appeared in the *Sun* of Saturday, the 6th of November. These pointed comments arose from the picture being *transparent*, and from a Circle, indicative of the strength and brotherly union of the Allies, which surmounted the same, composed of *gas* of brilliant brightness.

'The Two Kings of Terror': Napoleon mimicked by Death. This Rowlandson cartoon illustrated an account of the great Allied victory at Leipzig, 16-19 October 1813, which effectively cost the French control of Germany east of the Rhine.

Rhine between Coblenz and Mainz; while Schwarzenberg, 200,000 strong, headed for the Langres Plateau. At the rear, Bernadotte and Bennigsen set about containing Marshal Davout's well-led but isolated forces around Hamburg.

Meanwhile, defections continued. In early January Murat, King of Naples and Napoleon's own brother-in-law, came to an agreement with the Allies. Next, the King of Denmark deserted him. Paris itself was full of plotters seeking to insure themselves. The situation was all but hopeless, but Napoleon would not give up. As the Allies pushed back the cordon of barely seventy thousand troops who were defending the frontiers, he hastened his preparations for a campaign based upon the strategy of the 'Central Position' designed to safeguard the heart of what remained to him - Paris.

Selecting the Army of Silesia for his first effort, Napoleon failed to surprise Blücher at St Dizier. Pressing on, he fought a disappointing action at Brienne on 29 January only narrowly avoiding capture, which proved to be the prelude to a tactical defeat at La Rothière three days later. All in all, this represented a parlous opening for the French campaign, and Napoleon fell back on Troyes.

Fortunately, the Allies were bickering over permissible peace terms. As Napoleon set out to strike at the ponderous and over-extended Army of Bohemia, he learned that Blücher was again advancing on Paris along the Marne approach. Reordering his plans, the Emperor raced northwards to repulse the Army of Silesia, and in a series of staggering blows caught and defeated the over-extended Prussians and Russians in three battles in five days - Champaubert on 10 February, Montmirail on the 11th, and Vauchamps on the 14th.

These marvels Napoleon accomplished with only thirty thousand men - inflicting 20,000 casualties on an originally 50,000 strong opponent. Fortunately for Blücher, the arrival of General Winzingerode with a Russian corps of 30,000 men, fresh from the conquest of Belgium, saved the Army of Bohemia from complete eclipse, and enabled it to return to the offensive very quickly. But there was no denying that Napoleon's martial skill had again been demonstrated, and the morale of his tiny army soared.

Napoleon was now determined to mete out similar treatment to Schwarzenberg, currently near Montereau and Nogent on the Upper Seine, driving Marshals Victor, Oudinot and Macdonald before him. Paris - now very close to the southern front - gave itself over to a fit of panic. But Schwarzenberg could not maintain his impetus; attacked in the rear areas by infuriated French peasantry, worried about a French force near Lyons threatening his flank and, above all, apprehensive when he learned that Napoleon was heading south from the Marne, the Austrian hesitated. He had good reason. Within three days of disengaging from Blücher, Napoleon was near the Seine, and Schwarzenberg was fortunate to suffer only a serious repulse at Montereau on 17 February. The Allies fell back in disarray for Troyes.

Hopeful of success, Napoleon rejected another offer of peace terms, and set out to hound the Army of Bohemia with a total of 74,000 men, but the Allies destroyed so many bridges behind them that Blücher was able to join Schwarzenberg at Méry-sur-Seine on the 21st.

For a short time the Allies hesitated - but the Tsar and the King of Prussia were adamant that the campaign must be pressed to the conclusion. So Blücher was ordered back to the Marne while Schwarzenberg headed back through Troyes for Bar-sur-Aube and, ultimately, Langres. So ended a month of great French achievement, in which Napoleon had fully exploited the Allies' basic error of operating in two disunited armies. On the other hand, Napoleon was living on borrowed time.

The Allies made one last peace offer to Napoleon in early March, without success. Blücher, meanwhile, reinforced by Bülow's and Winzingerode's commands, was already advancing on Paris once more, pushing Marmont and Mortier before him near Meaux. Napoleon secretly moved north, and after a delay for bridge-building, crossed the Marne at La Ferté. Blücher had by then cautiously pulled back, and after crossing the Aisne, was heading for Laon, in order to join his reinforcements which brought his strength up to more than eight-five thousand.

Napoleon was still determined to close with this army, despite alarmist reports from Macdonald left in the south to the effect that Schwarzenberg was again moving forward, and had retaken Troyes on 4 March. The result was a considerable action at Craonne on 7 March, in which Ney and Mortier induced Blücher to withdraw his whole army to Laon.

There, on the 9th and 10th, was fought a second, very confused battle, where Marmont's VI Corps courted destruction but were able to escape because of the stalwart holding of the key Festieux defile by 125 soldiers of the Old Guard, and Napoleon was able to withdraw his remaining 42,000 men, after suffering 6,000 casualties. He had, nevertheless, been defeated, and gave orders for the fortifications of Paris to be readied. However, on 13 March Napoleon swept a force into Rheims behind Blücher, and this caused the Prussian to retire again on Laon. Schwarzenberg at once halted his advance over the Seine, and Napoleon seized the opportunity afforded by this hesitation, to transfer his exhausted troops southwards. In the nick of time, the Allies drew back towards Troyes once again.

Although he intended to strike towards St Dizier, Napoleon was also anxious to frighten off the Army of Bohemia. Accordingly, he headed for Arcis-sur-Aube, and there he engaged a substantial part of Schwarzenberg's 80,000 Allies with only 21,000 men on 20-21 March. In the end, the Emperor was again forced to break off the battle and retire over the Aube, heading for Sompuis to join Macdonald and Kellerman. Still believing that the game could be won, he headed for St Dizier, thus severing the Allied communications, on the 23rd. He was confident that this well-tried manœuvre would bring the enemy back, and thus away from Paris where the populace was in a state of great alarm as the Allies approached. For four days he waited, but there was still no sign of the enemy reacting as he hoped.

To his dismay, Napoleon gradually realised that his bluff had been called. The Allies continued to press on for Paris, ignoring Napoleon's presence in the rear, and by the 31st Mortier and Marmont were fighting on the Heights of Montmartre. Napoleon, bowing to the advice of his staff, headed for Paris. He had reached Fontainebleau on the 31st when he learned that Marmont had signed an armistice, and that the Allies were swarming into Paris. The Imperial family only just managed to slip away in time.

At Fontainebleau, a disappointed Emperor still talked of continuing the struggle, but on 2 April the Marshals, led by Ney, rebelled. 'The army will not march,' said Ney. Two days later, Napoleon had been persuaded to abdicate, first in favour of the King of Rome, then on 6 April, unconditionally. On 12 April, as the Allies decided what to do with him, Napoleon unsuccessfully tried to take poison. On the 16th the Allies announced that the Emperor would be ceded the tiny island of Elba, granted an allowance and allowed to keep a guard of 600 soldiers. His family were not, however, to join him. On 20 April Napoleon reviewed the Old Guard for the last time, and bade them farewell. Eight days later he boarded HMS *Undaunted* at St Raphael and sailed for exile. On the 30th the Bourbon King Louis XVIII, restored by the Allies to the

French throne, signed the Treaty of Paris, which restricted France to her frontiers of 1792. The long Napoleonic wars were at last over - or so it seemed.

The island of Elba contained Napoleon for not quite ten months. His friends in France kept him in close touch with developments, and he was soon aware that the Bourbons were becoming highly unpopular with the demobilised troops, and with the population as a whole; the peasantry in particular suspecting that the reactionaries desired to overthrow the Revolution's land settlement. All this Napoleon absorbed, and by late February 1815 he had made up his mind to risk one last grand gamble. On 1 March he landed near Cannes accompanied by a thousand followers and four guns. As the news was rushed to Paris and Vienna, where the Allied statesmen were meeting in Congress to try to reorder post-Napoleonic Europe, the Emperor set out for Grenoble. Louis XVIII sent troops to intercept him, but all deserted to their former leader, including Marshal Ney, who had taken service under the Bourbons. Napoleon's advance on Paris became a triumphal progress and on 19 March the Bourbons fled for Belgium. Next day, Napoleon re-entered the capital of Paris to the acclaim of the people. The Allies at Vienna declared Napoleon an outlaw on 27 March, and at once the Seventh Coalition was formed. England and Prussia agreed to put a force of 150,000 men into the field, and Austria and Russia promised another 400,000 by early July. Napoleon, meanwhile, hopeful that the Allies might recognise him as *de facto* ruler of France, started a 'peace offensive', but this soon failed. On 8 April he announced mobilisation, but reimposed the unpopular conscription only three weeks later. The 200,000 men taken over from the Bourbons were soon joined by seventy-five thousand loyal veterans and a further fifteen thousand volunteers; he hoped that a further 150,000 conscripts would have materialised within six months, but he could not afford to wait so long, for the Allies were already on the move, determined to invade France in great strength at three widely-separated points in July. Napoleon could choose between two strategies. Either he could wait with his forces near Paris and refight a campaign based on the rivers as in 1814, or he could launch a blow against the only enemies already in the field - namely Wellington and Blücher with their joint 209,000 men in the Netherlands region. He chose the latter course, not wishing to subject the French population to a repetition of 1814, and hopeful that a quick victory would break the Allied resolve. At the least it could bring down Lord Liverpool's British government.

'The Farewell at Fontainebleau'. After a last inspection of the Old Guard, Napoleon - who had recently abdicated unconditionally, sets out for exile on Elba, 20 April 1814.

In great secrecy, the French began to move 125,000 men towards the north-eastern frontiers, while French agents spied out the Allied dispositions. Napoleon planned to drive a wedge between the two enemy armies - after fooling Wellington with demonstrations towards the coast as if to threaten his communications with the Channel ports - before proceeding to defeat them in detail and

Failure, Exile and the Final Gamble

Napoleon reached Fontainebleau on 31 March only to learn that the Allies had occupied Paris. At last his marshals rebelled. 'The Army will not march', declared Ney, their spokesman. 'The Army will obey me.' 'The Army will obey its chiefs'. The nadir of the First Empire had been reached. Napoleon abdicated on 6 April and attempted suicide six days later, unsuccessfully. On 20 April he was on his way to Elba.

thereafter occupying Brussels. To command his army, Napoleon chose the repentant Ney, a great hero with the rank and file, Grouchy, a competent cavalry commander and Soult as Chief of Staff. Berthier had recently died under mysterious circumstances at Bamberg, and Murat's offer of aid had been rejected, but the able Davout was appointed Governor of Paris - a key political post. From 7 June all the frontiers of France were sealed for security. The previous day, the five French corps, the Imperial Guard and the Reserve Cavalry had begun to move from their scattered locations towards the designated concentration area around Beaumont, not far from Charleroi and the Belgian frontier.

On the 14th Napoleon reached Beaumont. Next day, the French *Armée du Nord* advanced to the Sambre in three columns, the left under Ney, the right under Grouchy and the central reserve under Napoleon in person, and crossed into Belgium. The Allies were taken almost wholly by surprise, and Wellington's first reaction was to order his army to move west of Brussels towards Mons in the belief that Napoleon would attempt to envelop his right flank.

Blücher, who had realised that something was afoot the previous day, ordered his army to concentrate forward around Fleurus, right in the path of the French right wing. The Allies thus obligingly drew apart rather than together.

The immediate French aim was to master the road running through Quatre Bras down to Sombreffe - practically the only Allied line of lateral communication. Which enemy they would fight first would depend on circumstances. By late on the 15th Ney was within sight of Quatre Bras when the appearance of a small Allied force, whose commander had intelligently disregarded

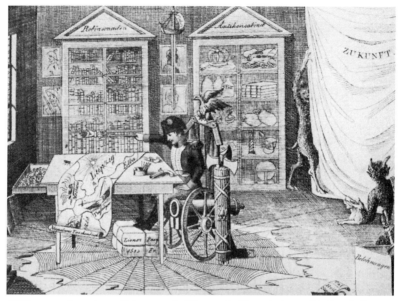

With a naval version of 'the sword of Damocles' hanging over his head, the sorcerer studies the series of disasters that have led him to Elba, whilst two familiars draw the curtains on his career. In fact, this verdict was to prove a trifle premature.

Napoleon's dramatic return to France on 1 March 1815, led to the precipitate flight of Louis XVIII, whose crown topples from his head.

On 10 March, Napoleon reached Lyons. By this time the initially cautious welcome that had met his return had given place to a warm greeting, and his march on Paris became a triumphal progress.

Wellington's order to move west, convinced him that Wellington was hidden with his main army nearby. He accordingly halted. On the other flank, Grouchy had fought against an advanced Prussian corps for most of the day and pressed it back to Fleurus. This was the situation by nightfall.

It was while attending the Duchess of Richmond's ball at Brussels that night that Wellington realised that he had been fooled. At once he issued new orders summoning his army towards Quatre Bras, but he was aware that he would be fortunate to assemble enough men to fend off Ney if the Marshal attacked early enough in sufficient force. The Allied Reserve, General Picton's 5th Division, was however still at Brussels. As for Blücher, he continued to order his four corps to mass near Fleurus on the morrow. Realising that this was the case,

Arthur Wellesley, Duke of Wellington. After mastering the French armies in Portugal and Spain, he set the seal on his fine military reputation by defeating Napoleon himself at Waterloo.

Napoleon decided to try conclusions with the Prussian first. Ney was to capture and hold Quatre Bras while the Emperor joined Grouchy to defeat Blücher. Thereafter, Napoleon would swing his reserve to reinforce Ney for a decisive trial of strength with Wellington. The omens appeared propitious.

The 16th therefore saw two battles about seven miles apart. By 2.30 pm the Emperor and Grouchy were in action against Blücher's 84,000 men at Ligny, one corps still being on the road from Liège. Ney had attacked at Quatre Bras about half an hour earlier, very belatedly, considering his proximity to the skeleton forces facing him, and this delay had enabled Wellington to reinforce the position to eight thousand men and sixteen guns, with many more on the way. It would be a race against time, but six hours had been gained thanks to Ney's inactivity throughout the morning.

Blücher was soon under heavy pressure to the east, but Napoleon needed Ney's second corps to clinch the battle by appearing on the Prussian right flank. Orders were accordingly sent, but through a series of confusions Ney countermanded General d'Erlon's move, and the I Corps consequently took no part in either battle on the 16th - though its presence at either would have been decisive. This muddle reduced the scale of the defeat inflicted on the Prussians by nightfall, and also enabled Wellington to achieve parity and then superiority over Ney at Quatre Bras. Still, Napoleon had defeated one adversary and checked the other, and he expected to see Wellington destroyed the next day. A fatal error, however, was his belief that the Prussians were retreating towards Namur and Liège along their communications. In fact, by better luck than judgment, they were retreating north towards Wavre, and thus were keeping in contact with Wellington. Blücher, who had been unhorsed in the battle, was saved by

Field Marshal Blücher, 'Alte Vorwärts' ('Old Forwards') to his men, who also dubbed him 'Papa', proved an inveterate opponent of Napoleon. Despite his advanced years, and the rough handling he received at Ligny on 16 June 1815, he was insistent that his army should march to reinforce Wellington at Waterloo.

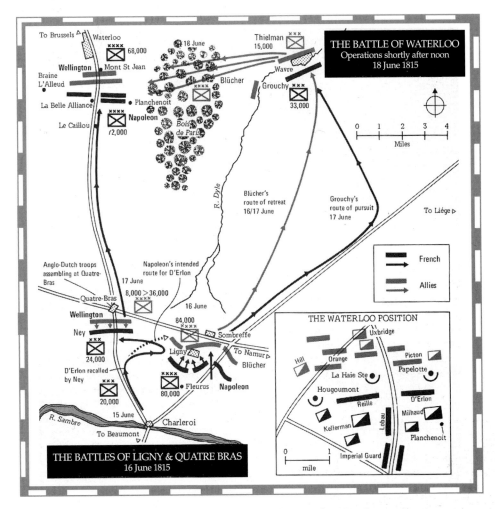

To Brussels   Waterloo
Wellington   Mont St Jean   68,000
18 June
Braine
L'Alleud
La Belle Alliance   Planchenoit
Le Caillou   Napoleon   Bois de Paris   72,000

Thielman   15,000
Wavre
Blücher
Grouchy   33,000

THE BATTLE OF WATERLOO
Operations shortly after noon
18 June 1815

0   1   2   3   4
Miles

Blücher's
route of retreat
16/17 June

Grouchy's
route of pursuit
17 June

To Liége

Anglo-Dutch troops
assembling at Quatre-
Bras
Quatre-Bras
Wellington
Ney   24,000
D'Erlon recalled
by Ney   20,000

Napoleon's intended
route for D'Erlon
17 June
8,000 > 36,000
16 June
84,000
Ligny   Sombreffe
To Namur
Blücher
Fleurus   Napoleon
80,000

R. Sambre   15 June   Charleroi
To Beaumont

French

Allies

THE WATERLOO POSITION

Uxbridge
Hill   Orange   Picton
La Haie Ste   Papelotte
Hougoumont
Reille   D'Erlon
Kellerman   Lobau   Milhaud
Planchenoit

0   1
mile   Imperial Guard

THE BATTLES OF LIGNY & QUATRE BRAS
16 June 1815

an aide and restored to his army later that night. His determination to sustain his ally Wellington would be of great importance to the outcome of this campaign, for his Chief of Staff, Gneisenau, would have preferred to head for the Rhine at once.

On the 17th, the Emperor, who was far from well, failed to order a full pursuit of the Prussians until after midday. This serious oversight was compounded by Ney, who also wasted the whole morning. As a result, instead of being pinned to Quatre Bras, Wellington was able to thin out his forces progressively and retire towards the ridge of Mont St Jean. He had received assurances by this time that Blücher would aid him on the morrow. When

Napoleon at last realised that his chance of trapping Wellington was fast receding, it proved too late to catch the Allies. Although Ney was hounded into action, to find himself facing only a rearguard, and Napoleon raced his reserves across country to try to intercept the retreat, he failed to catch Wellington, for heavy rain hindered the French more than the Allies, who were using the main road from Charleroi to Brussels. By evening, therefore, Wellington had reached his intended position at Mont St Jean (he had selected it as a possible battleground some time earlier), and there turned at bay. The French, after assuring themselves that Wellington was in fact present in force, turned in for the night in the pouring rain, two miles to the south. The scene was set for the battle of Waterloo.

Wellington's position was strong. His force was posted in the main behind a three-mile ridge, bisected by the highway; to the front, three strongpoints had been occupied, La Haie Sainte in the centre, Hougoumont Château to the right, Papelotte on the left. A substantial force was left to the west of the battlefield near Braine l'Alleud in case the French attempted a characteristic outflanking movement. On the battlefield itself, he deployed 68,000 British and Allied troops and 184 guns, with great strength on his right: for he expected the Prussians to reinforce his left. His strategy would be to cling on grimly to his positions until Blücher could move forces from Wavre to his aid. Napoleon did not take this possibility seriously, though Grouchy had reported the Prussians to be at Wavre late on the 17th.

Owing to a wet night, Napoleon could position his 266 guns only after 10 am, and so his 72,000 men were in position only by midday. By the time his great battery of eight-four guns was drawn up before his right centre, Napoleon had placed Reille's II Corps on the left, supported by Kellermann's and Guyot's cavalry; d'Erlon's I Corps, sustained by Milhaud's and Lefebvre-Desnouette's horsemen, held the right; and in central reserve a little to the rear stood Lobau's VI Corps and the Imperial Guard. The Emperor's plan lacked subtlety, revealing his misplaced contempt for his opponent, the 'Sepoy General'. Reille was to mount a diversionary attack against Hougoumont, designed to draw in Wellington's reserves and weaken the Allied centre, which would then be the target for a crushing main attack led by d'Erlon's troops. He was confident that nightfall would find him in Brussels. Almost inexplicably, considering Ney's inadequate performance over the past two days, Napoleon appointed the Marshal to command the fighting.

The battle of Borodino (also known as the Moskova), 7 September 1812. Marshal Berthier returns the sword of a Russian general while General Caulaincourt storms the Great Redout.

Napoleon's sometime Grande Armée melted away during the dreadful march through the Russian winter in 1812, and during the equally hard campaign in Germany the next year. Nevertheless, the early months of 1814 found the Emperor still at the head of a scratch and outnumbered enemy, defending the soil of France from the invaders. Painting - 'Napoleon's Retreat From Moscow' - by Adolf Northern.

At 11.30 am Prince Jérôme Bonaparte led forward his division to attack Hougoumont. Very soon this operation ran into difficulties near the orchard, protected by a stout wall, and the headstrong Jerome summoned more and more men until about two divisions of Reille's four were tied down, and remained so all day. The château, though ultimately on fire, never fell, and Wellington had to send the equivalent of only two battalions to its aid. Thus the secondary attack misfired seriously for the French.

Meantime, Grouchy had attacked the Prussians at Wavre instead of heading for Waterloo - hoping to keep Blücher's forces pinned down. In this, his thirty-three thousand men were unsuccessful for it took only a single corps of fifteen thousand Prussians to contain the French, while Blücher marched through the muddy forests towards his ally with all of 89,000 troops.

About 1.30 pm Napoleon first received news of the leading Prussians' approach and he sent an order to Grouchy, requiring him to march to his aid, but this order was too late to be practicable. He still believed that he had plenty of time to win the victory. Forward, at Ney's order, went the I Corps in four great columns, but unsupported by cavalry or horse artillery. As it breasted the slope, it was first checked by the fire of Picton's division, and then flung back in ruin by the charge of the Union Brigade led by the Royal Scots Greys. However, this force would not rally, but charged the Grand Battery before being routed in disorder by French lancers. Nevertheless, Wellington's line had held.

The Grand Battery had gone into action about 1 pm, but the wetness of the ground had impaired the damage caused by the shot, and only a single brigade, left atop the ridge, took heavy casualties. Thus Wellington was still unshaken in his position while Napoleon had already decided to send the VI Corps to form a defensive flank to the east, ready to meet the approaching Prussians. The French were losing the initiative.

Ney next tried to take La Haie Sainte in the centre, but was driven back shortly after 3.30 pm. However, he believed that he had detected signs of an Allied withdrawal in the centre, and at once ordered Milhaud's cavalry to charge. In fact, he had seen ambulances going to the rear, with a few fugitives, and so his horsemen found Wellington's line transformed into twenty fire-fringed and bayonet-bristling squares. Ney had failed to send forward horse artillery to support the cavalry, so they were pounded by the British gunners and infantry. More and more French cavalry became attracted to the action - on whose order is still uncertain - and in all, a dozen charges were made over the narrow sector of ground between La Haie Sainte and Hougoumont, without decisive effect, for the ground was not only confined but also so muddy that it slowed the attacks to trotting pace. Eventually, Napoleon, aghast at Ney's misuse of the cavalry, had to send the remaining squadrons to extricate the survivors. Another chance of victory was therefore missed, once again through Ney's failure to use properly-balanced forces of mixed troops. And Wellington had won still more invaluable time for Blücher to arrive.

By 4 pm Lobau was fighting against Prussians on the French right, the struggle centring around Planchenoit which changed hands several times. Napoleon had to send part of the Guard to retake the village, while the remainder drew up east of the main road in a support line. Thus almost all French reserves were now committed.

On Napoleon's order, at 6 pm, Ney again attacked La Haie Sainte - this time with a properly constituted force, and because of this, and the defenders running short of ammunition, the attack succeeded. Two French batteries were soon pouring shot into Wellington's wavering centre at point-blank range, and the crisis of the day had come. But when Ney, at last sensing victory, appealed to his master for reserves, he received a brusque answer. The Guard was already deployed, and no other reserves were available. Thus the last real chance of victory passed.

By 7 pm two corps of Prussians were steadily pressing the French back from Planchenoit, and a third was coming into view behind Wellington's left wing. In a desperate and deliberately mendacious attempt to rally his men's flagging morale, Napoleon had the word spread that this force was, in fact, Grouchy come to outflank the Allies. At the same time, Napoleon was reassembling part of the Guard in reserve and about 7.15 pm he sent Ney the Middle Guard for a last attempt at a breakthrough. The veterans advanced in a number of columns, but for some reason veered away from the main road, and then breasted the slope towards Wellington's right centre. Both armies held their breath - the Guard had never failed in its eleven years of existence. This time, however, the seven battalions that reached the crest were met by point-blank infantry fire by Chassé's brigade and Maitland's British Guards, together with Adam's brigade. In ten minutes it was all over, and the French unbelievingly witnessed the Guard in retreat. At the same time, the latest Prussian arrivals opened cannon fire on the French, and the soldiers, fearing that Grouchy might have changed sides, sent up

Napoleon at the battle of Jena, 14 October 1806. With his customary informality with his soldiers, he turns to acknowledge the salutation by a grenadier of the Imperial Guard. The ensuing double-success of Jena-Auerstädt made Napoleon undisputed master of Central Europe.

The defeated Napoleon takes shelter within a steady square formed by a battalion of Grenadiers of the Old Guard, 'the oldest of the old'. This élite formation did a great deal to delay the Allied pursuit, and added further lustre to its reputation in this, its last action.

the cry of 'treason' and then 'save yourselves.'

The French army disintegrated into a horde of fugitives, but the Old Guard added further lustre to its name by its steady retreat, covering the flight of the rest. For a time, the Emperor stayed with one of the retiring squares, but later transferred to his coach, then to his horse, and eventually reached safety. Soon after, Grouchy was also retreating in good order, but Wellington and Blücher, who met near La Belle Alliance, had won a devastating victory. This was all the more amazing considering that many of Wellington's troops were not of first-line quality (most of his Peninsular veterans were over the Atlantic in Canada and the United States taking part in a

The meeting of Wellington and Blücher late on 18 June 1815, at the farm of La Belle Alliance. Blücher wanted to give this name to the battle, but Wellington insisted on Waterloo - the site of his rear headquarters about two miles north of Mont St. Jean where the actual fighting took place.

separate war, and many of the Dutch and Belgian formations making up his army were of questionable quality) while Napoleon's army had been made up almost wholly of veterans. However, the choice of questionable senior commanders, an army filled with doubts about their comrades' loyalty and the loss of irreplaceable time on the morning of the 18th had contributed towards Napoleon's last defeat. The price was 33,000 casualties and 220 guns lost; or 60,000 since the 15th; the Allies, on the other hand, had lost 22,000 men at Waterloo, including Prussians, or 55,000 since the short campaign began. But whereas the Allies, with Austrians and Russians moving to their aid, could absorb their losses, France could not. Napoleon's gamble had undeniably failed.

Napoleon still spoke of retrieving the situation as the Allies became increasingly strung out in their new advance on Paris, but his credibility was gone. Not even his ministers would support him, and on 22 June Napoleon was persuaded to abdicate for the second, and final time. There was still some fighting outside Paris, where Davout acquitted himself well at the head of 117,000 troops, but Napoleon's meteoric career was over. On 3 July he left for Rochefort, planning to escape to the United States, but the Royal Navy were blockading the port. On the 15th he agreed to board HMS *Bellerophon,* hoping that the British Prince Regent would afford him a sanctuary in England. But this was not to be. Without setting foot in the land of his mortal foe, he was shipped to exile on the rocky South Atlantic Isle of St Helena.

Six years of exile at Longwood followed. The conditions of his virtual imprisonment were embittered by the callous severity of the Governor, Sir Hudson Lowe. The former Emperor soon despaired of the Allies' allowing his family to join him - Marie-Louise had returned to Austria, and his son, the new Duke of Reichstadt, was kept at Vienna (until his premature death in 1832). Napoleon spent the weary years, attended by a small staff, in contemplation and in dictating his memoirs. Eventually his health deteriorated, and on 5 May 1821 Napoleon Bonaparte died. So ended one of the most eventful and dramatic lives in human history.

If the years had been dominated by war after war which will for ever remain the first mental association when Napoleon's name is mentioned, the constructive side of his genius - in codes of law and a reorganised Europe - must also be taken into account, for Napoleon has left a lasting imprint on history, for both good and bad, and this will never wholly be erased by time.

CHAPTER SIX

Napoleon and his Art of War

'**M**en of genius are meteors destined to be consumed in illuminating their century', wrote Napoleon as a young man in 1790. His own career - from first emergence at Toulon to final cataclysm at Waterloo - spanned twenty-two action-packed and dynamic years of European history, the results of which are still very much part of the pattern of life and institutions over a century and a half later. Napoleon was more than a remarkable soldier and an outstanding statesman: he was a born and natural leader of men. This quality of leadership is fundamental to any understanding of his generalship and, indeed, lay at its foundation. It made his troops follow him where they would have followed no one else; it made his marshals accept orders which they would have questioned from a lesser man; it made his adopted countrymen

Napoleon at Wagram 1809. The Emperor exercised close personal command at all his greatest battles, carefully timing the opening of the successive phases.

fight as they had never fought before - and would never fight again.

Napoleon's personal magnetism is not to be explained in physical terms. Of small stature, inclined to stoutness from early middle age, he was a sitting target for hostile caricaturists such as Rowlandson, Gillray or Terebenev. Even in the years of Napoleon's youth, Lasalle recorded that he 'looked more like a mathematician than a general', and in 1796 his sharp features and sallow complexion, unsteady gait and neglected clothing attracted some initial ridicule. Nothing could have been further from the truth than Canova's celebrated classical statue of Napoleon, which portrays him as a god-like being of more than human size. Nevertheless, all who met him were instantly struck by his natural authority and above all by his large, greyish-blue, deep-seated eyes which had an almost hypnotic effect. In manner he could be charming, considerate, crude or in turn, vulgar, and almost invariably outspoken, yet he had it in his power to place in thrall the soul of almost any man or woman he encountered. 'So it is that I, who fear neither God nor Devil, am ready to tremble like a child when I approach him,' confided the war-hardened General Vandamme.

This hypnotic fascination undoubtedly accounts for much of the mastery he exerted over all his subjects, both military and civil. Once exercised, this power could transcend both time and space, though Napoleon learned in 1812 that the loyalty it produced was limited to his person alone; the Malet conspiracy, based upon an unfounded but half-expected announcement that the Emperor had perished in Russia, threw the French government into confusion for several days, and hardly any ministers or high civil servants rallied to Napoleon's heir, the infant King of Rome. Nevertheless, this magnetism formed a powerful weapon in his armoury, and Napoleon made deliberate and systematic use of it on many an occasion to obtain his way. 'If I want a man sufficiently badly,' he remarked during the Consulate, 'I would kiss his arse.' The easy familiarity which he permitted the rank and file made him highly popular. Many of his methods were deliberately theatrical. He encouraged the men to present in person their claims to promotion or a decoration, and used his knack for remembering the faces and records of old soldiers to spread a little more of his charisma among the men during his unending inspections. The lightest rebuke could reduce a veteran grenadier to tears; the merest passing word would be treasured by the recipient for life. The ultimate accolade for a soldier was to have the Emperor seize the lobe of his ear between

Napoleon, accompanied by a small staff, on board HMS Bellerophon on the first stage of his journey into final exile. Ahead lay the island of St Helena.

thumb and forefinger and give it a good tweak.

Tales of personal recognition of this type were legion, but, although no doubt many an old soldier exaggerated his own greatest moment, there is no need to query the truth of most of the stories. Within hours of boarding the British man-of-war HMS *Bellerophon* off Rochefort in 1815, Napoleon had completely won over both officers and crew. In the sad, final years of exile, only one man proved wholly unsusceptible to the former Emperor's charm - the oafish Sir Hudson Lowe, Governor of St Helena, an undistinguished soldier who exasperated his fellow-countrymen almost as much as he infuriated his distinguished captive. Few other foreigners who met him were so resistant - so there is small wonder that his effect on his own men was so electric.

Just as his personality set him apart from other men so also did the incredible range and sheer power of his intellectual capabilities. Octave Aubry, the historian, wrote that Napoleon possessed 'the greatest personality of all time, superior to other men of action by virtue of the range and clarity of his intelligence, his speed of decision, his unswerving determination, and his acute sense of reality, allied to the imagination on which great minds thrive.' The Emperor's interests were not restricted to purely professional matters - they were many, embracing the arts and sciences, jurisprudence and economics, education and industry.

His fertile mind was rarely at a loss for a valuable idea on practically any subject, and he possessed to a marked degree the ability to study every facet of a subject without losing sight of the central, most significant aspect. His grasp of detail was phenomenal, his powers of concentration daunting; yet he could switch from one avenue of thought to another at a moment's notice without in the least clouding his incisive mind. He once summarised his mental agility as follows: 'Different subjects and different affairs are arranged in my head as in a cupboard. When I wish to interrupt one train of thought, I shut that drawer and open another. Do I wish to sleep? I simply close all the drawers, and there I am - asleep.' When dictating letters in those pre-shorthand days, he was capable of keeping four secretaries hard at work on as many different subjects, pacing from one to the next in turn to rattle off a sentence without once confusing his various trains of thought. He could assimilate information at a glance, and retain it in his near-photographic memory, which was particularly receptive to statistics. Many a minister or secretary of state was astounded by his mastery of departmental business, and it was practically impossible to conceal errors or shortcomings when faced by Napoleon's razor-sharp mind and ruthless scrutiny.

Behind everything lay Napoleon's phenomenal capacity for hard and unremitting toil. 'Work is my element,' he once asserted. 'I was born and made for work. I have recognised the limits of my eye-sight and of my legs, but never the limits of my working-power.' On another occasion he remarked that he worked at meal-times, when attending the opera, even in bed. A twenty-hour day was nothing extraordinary for him, and he worked his perspiring teams of secretaries and servants almost to death. Even in the boiling-hot baths which constituted one of his few luxuries, he would hold interviews, liberally splashing his impeccably-attired visitors as they sweltered amid the clouds of steam. Alternatively, he would summon one of his intimates to read to him from state papers or, more rarely, some novel.

On campaign his routine was arduous in the extreme. He was a hard task-master, but drove no one harder than himself. He habitually retired to his camp-bed at 8 or 9 pm of an evening for

Cartoon depicting the price of 'la gloire'. Every year tens of thousands of conscripts were enlisted only to be sacrificed to the ravages of disease and the flames of war. This 'blood-tax' became increasingly unpopular with both the French people and their allies.

four hours' sleep. Rising at midnight, he read the latest reports from the corps commanders on the previous day's events, dictated the necessary replies, issued any changes of orders and then retired shortly before dawn for a further hour's sleep. By six in the morning, he would have dressed and breakfasted, and the main work of the day could begin. First he would summon General Bacler d'Albe with his maps, and together they would crawl on all fours over them, measuring distances and driving in coloured marking-pins, red and black, as they considered future movements. Next, the Emperor would often grant interviews to important personages summoned to the presence or desirous of seeing him personally. Sometimes they had to wait in the antechamber for days on end before receiving an interview. These matters completed, Napoleon entered his office and went to his desk. There stacks of sorted documents would be awaiting his attention, the Emperor scrawling brief minutes in the margins of reports, dictating a quick letter to one of his secretaries, or simply flinging papers onto the floor if he deemed them unworthy of his attention. More dictation and brief interviews followed, and by ten o'clock the new letters and despatches would be back on his desk awaiting signature. A hasty glance through their contents, and a scrawled 'N' at the foot would be sufficient to send most of them on their way. But when a matter of grave importance was involved, Napoleon would place the document on one side with the remark: 'Until tomorrow; night

'Here is the best-cooked one, my Emperor'. Napoleon's ceaseless inspections-both formal and informal-enabled him to gauge the moral of his troops. He allowed the rank and file almost limitless familiarity, and knew how to inspire heroic efforts.

Napoleon's camp-bed, preserved in the Musée de L' Armée in Paris. The bed curtains and hangings are green.

brings counsel.'

    After completing his routine business, the Emperor would call for his horse and set off accompanied by his 'little headquarters' to inspect a unit or visit a senior headquarters. He was firmly convinced of the importance of a commander-in-chief seeing and being seen, and the incessant inspections, reviews and parades gave him the opportunity of assessing the morale and mettle of his men. On days of battle, he would issue the grand tactical orders to his generals and then leave them to get on with the job, leaving him free to watch the crucial timings, the positioning and deployment of reserves and the correlation of messages and reports from the various sectors. He would also ride among the ranks waiting to move into action, cheering and inspiring them with his words, and so heedless of his own safety that at one critical moment of the battle of Aspern-Essling in 1809 the Imperial Guard threatened to

'The last brew'. A cartoon shows Blücher (left) and Wellington (right), aided by an allegorical triple-headed monster (probably representing the Allies-Russia, Austria and Sweden) disposing of the last French troops in 1815.

Poking satirical fun at the fallen Emperor. He is depicted giving a constitution and exacting an oath from the rats on the island of St Helena, the scene of his last exile.

ground arms *'si l'empereur ne se retire pas'*. On other occasions, when feeling off-form or ill, as at Borodino, Napoleon would spend the entire day in the rear taking scant interest in what was taking place, merely doubting the authenticity of every report, and refusing to release reserves - but such episodes were rare.

After returning from the day's ride, Napoleon returned to his desk to read the latest news and digests, taking action as necessary. For information he drew upon his *carnets* (or notebooks of carefully up-dated information), Savary's spy reports and the *résumés* prepared by Berthier's staff. His perspiring secretaries found it difficult to keep up with the speed of their master's dictation, as Napoleon paced up and down the room or tent, his racing mind devising complicated reports or march timetables for half a dozen corps without effort.

Meals were at the best of times haphazard affairs. A frugal luncheon was normally taken in the saddle or with the officer of a unit he was visiting, but the timing of the evening meal was rarely consistent. Nevertheless, the Emperor expected food to be ready the moment he decided to eat, and the imperial cooks often found themselves preparing and discarding endless meals while awaiting their master's pleasure. Napoleon rarely dined alone; he usually sat down with Berthier, or, in his absence, with other close associates or

Napoleon 'the little' furiously upbraids a very ruffled French eagle,
symbolising his armies in Spain, for being mastered by the British.

distinguished visitors to his headquarters. His servants recorded that Napoleon ate quickly - twenty minutes being the average time for a meal - and as often as not in silence; he ate little, and drank even less, but was partial to an occasional glass of his favourite Chambertin.

After-dinner relaxation was rare, but sometimes the Emperor would call for cards and play an uproarious game of pontoon or whist, cheating extensively and consequently always emerging the winner. Under normal conditions, after a final conference with Bacler d'Albe, the Emperor retired to his camp-bed in mid-evening, but even then the harassed 'household' could hardly relax, for at any moment the well-known voice would be heard calling for an aide or a secretary to take dictation.

His relations with his officers and staff were often very strained. Napoleon believed that the way to screw the maximum effort out of his officers was to keep them in a state bordering on nervous anxiety. Normally his mood was fair and just, but nobody could ever be sure that one of those redoubtable rages or one of his equally-feared fits of severity was not imminent. He rationed his smiles and jokes, and had few favourites. He often played his subordinates - particularly the marshals - off against one another, adopting the maxim of Caligula: *'divide et impera'*. He expected instant obedience and would tolerate nothing less. Even Berthier, who was permitted more familiarity than anyone else, was occasionally driven to near-despair by the performance of his duties under the ever-critical and rarely-satisfied eye of his master. 'I am being killed by hard work,' he once lamented in 1812, 'a mere soldier is happier than I.'

Napoleon's labours certainly imposed an immense strain on his resources. 'I am today at Gera, my dearest love,' he wrote in one revealing letter to Josephine in October 1806, shortly before Jena-Auerstadt, 'and things are going very well . . . My health remains excellent, and I have put on weight since my departure. Yet I travel from 20 to 25 leagues a day, on horseback, in my carriage etc., I retire to rest at eight o'clock and rise at midnight. I sometimes imagine that you will not have yet retired to bed.' Yet we know that Napoleon's physique was not as tough as it has sometimes been represented. His valets reveal that he needed regular sleep, even if the amount was limited. However, he had the happy knack of being able to cat-nap at odd moments of the day; even amid the din of Wagram in 1809, he stretched himself out on his bearskin rug for a short sleep. He was quite frequently ill, suffering persistently from both piles and bladder-trouble, and ill-health had a bearing on his showing at both Borodino and Waterloo. His irregular eating habits affected his digestion, but he never seems to have suffered from insomnia.

At a time of crisis, he could work for between two and three days without real pause, although the toll was felt later on. Between 18 and 19 September 1806, for example, Napoleon is known to have dictated no less than 102 orders and letters to his staff, working in relays, in effect launching a complete campaign in all its planning and administrative aspects. Clearly, Napoleon possessed immense reserves of nervous energy to make such feats possible, but beneath the calm surface great passions lurked, which sometimes led to tearing rages which his intimates had reason to fear. He would not hesitate to use his riding-crop on the heads and shoulders of officers and servants, and at least once he kicked a minister in the crutch. On another occasion, he seized poor Berthier by the throat and hammered his head against a stone wall until the paroxysm subsided. Normally, however, he retained strict control over his emotions, using them as instruments to his will. Nevertheless there are those who subscribe to the belief that he suffered from hystero-epilepsy, the so-called 'conqueror's syndrome'.

Whatever the views of enemy propaganda or critics, he was no monster. Basically he was endowed with much the same qualities and faults as any other human being, but of course the additional unique circumstances of his genius and opportunities increased the scope and impact of these upon others far beyond the normal limits. He probably wielded more power than any man in pre-twentieth-century history, but it is amazing how much time elapsed before he succumbed to its temptations. Throughout his career, indeed, he was more interested in the accumulation of the *means* of power than in its unbridled employment; on most occasions, he was moderate in its use, although he could also be utterly ruthless.

He always stressed that he was a realist, but there was also a strong streak of fatalism in his make-up. 'All that is to happen is written down. Our hour is marked and we cannot prolong it a minute longer than fate has proclaimed.' This fatalistic attitude crystallised into a belief in his being set apart from the mass of humanity, though in the end his 'sense of destiny' affected his judgment as a realist and led to the irrational obstinacy of the last years of his decline and fall.

This, then, was the personality which captivated a generation of Frenchmen. Added to it was an extraordinary, if limited, military

'The presentation of the Eagles at Versailles in 1810'. These insignia symbolised the Emperor's personal connection with every regiment, and they became the focal points for resistance and valour in many a battle. Several versions were issued, the original 'lozenge' shape of the tricolor being converted into the more familiar horizontal format early in 1815.

talent which ensured his immortality as one of the truly great generals of modern history.

One outstanding element of this talent was sheer professional mastery. Trained as a gunner, in later life he claimed that he could still cast both cannon and shot, manufacture gunpowder and construct carriages and limbers. This interest in the *minutiae* of military affairs was part of his quest for perfect thoroughness, but it must be admitted that he had his blind-spots. He never, for instance, appreciated the full influence of winds and tides on naval operations. It can also be argued that he took an insufficient interest in minor tactics during the years of his prime. At St Helena, he was adamant that a two-deep linear formation was ideal for infantry, but he had never suggested its adoption in any of his earlier battles.

Napoleon once listed the three basic requirements for successful generalship: namely, concentration of force, activity and a firm resolve to perish gloriously. 'They are the three principles of the military art that have disposed luck in my favour in all my operations. Death is nothing, but to live defeated is to die every day...' - as, indeed, was destined to be his own fate. A fourth principle of importance might be added to these three, and occurs again and again in the Emperor's letters and despatches - the importance of surprising the enemy at both the strategic and tactical levels of warfare.

Utilising his great mental powers, he was in the habit of thinking through any military problem days, even months, in advance. This process of concentrated analysis was no light affair and Napoleon once likened the effort involved to that of a woman bringing a child into the world. He invariably thought a problem through to the very bottom and examined it from every side, taking every foreseeable possibility into account and making allowance for every conceivable complication. Even then he was not satisfied, but must leave some space for pure chance, which he gave a mathematical position in his calculations. Thus most of his seemingly inspirational and opportunist adjustments of plans in mid-campaign were in fact pre-considered concepts, and it was rare for a situation to find him completely at a loss.

Napoleon was also positive that 'a military leader must possess as much character as intellect - the base must equal the height'. He was liberally endowed in both respects. He was also convinced that 'a general's principal talent consists in knowing the mentality of the soldier and in gaining his confidence'. At this, too, as we have seen, he was a past master. He knew the strengths and weaknesses of the

French soldier to the last detail, from his courage 'of an impatient sort' when matters were going well, to his tendency to become disproportionately dejected after failure. He mastered most of the psychological aspects of man-management very early in his career. The secret was the judicious combination of stick and carrot. Battle-honours, swords of honour, promotions, titles, decorations and financial rewards were lavishly bestowed on the deserving. Those who let him down without good reason were mercilessly castigated. 'Quartermaster-General,' the young General declaimed before two recalcitrant units of the Army of Italy in 1796, 'let it be inscribed on their colours: "They no longer belong to the Army of Italy".' Penalties of this type were bitterly regretted by the recipients, and any steps would be taken to persuade the Emperor to retract his view and restore the troops concerned to favour. He was thus pre-eminent in the skills of practical generalship as well as in the theoretical planning of great concepts.

Centralisation of supreme authority was another vital tenet of Napoleon's command philosophy. 'In war men are nothing; one man is everything'; or again, 'better one bad general than two good ones'. The degree of centralisation which he required - and achieved - was fantastic. Practically every decision was taken, or at least approved, by the Emperor in person, and his contemporaries marvelled that he continued to attempt to run a war and a continental-sized Empire at the same time. So long as his armies remained of manageable proportions, his unique command methods functioned surprisingly well; the French corps marched over Europe in a well co-ordinated pattern, the whole being directed by a single master-intelligence. In the later years, however, the desire for rigid centralisation became a snare and a delusion.

Behind everything else lay Napoleon's boundless ambition. This, allied to great and ruthless ability, formed a fertile breeding-ground for both achievements and disaster. For many years Napoleon followed a worthy inspiration; only latterly did the ideal he set himself become tarnished.

Every human quality unfortunately has its perversion, and as the years of near limitless power passed, Napoleon's abilities began to atrophy or produce sad distortions. Censorship of press, pulpit and salon, the apparatus of police terror wielded by Fouché, and the very growth of the Empire's boundaries - all are evidence of incipient megalomania. The Emperor's ambition became increasingly self-centred. The unscrupulous treatment of the Spanish royal family at Bayonne, the earlier execution of Enghien, the humiliation of Prince Hatzfeld at Berlin in 1806, the shoddy treatment of the King of Prussia at Tilsit - all were indications of growing tyranny. Even his allies were treated with condescension and without tact - for Napoleon had always been out-spoken in his views. This lack of what Bismarck called 'the golden quality of statesmanship' made it impossible for him to convert an ex-enemy into a convinced ally, however great the personal charm he could exert when he chose. Every ally was forced to accept the status of a vassal; every defeated foe was converted into a resentful satellite. Napoleon's price for his favours was ever high. Even Bernadotte was turned into an active foe.

The same lack of tact encouraged him in adopting illogical and extreme vendettas. The struggle with Britain took on all the irrational overtones of a Mafia feud. This led Napoleon into making his two cardinal errors of grand strategy - the declaration of all-out economic warfare in late 1806, which rebounded upon his own head with a vengeance, and ultimately drove him towards those fatal military involvements with Spain and Russia.

In the last years, irrationality increased. Even in early 1814 when the cards were clearly on the table, he refused to accept the inevitable, or even to acknowledge the utter exhaustion of French resources and the weariness of the people. As difficulties multiplied, he tended to blame his subordinates. This latent distrust of his assistants was an important factor in his political and military decline as evidenced in the previous chapter.

The strains, year on year, of remorseless war told on his own personality and skill as well as upon the marshalate. Once, in a flash of insight, he had acknowledged this: 'Ordner is worn out,' he declared in 1805. 'One only has a certain time for war. I have another six years in me, then I shall have to stop.' Here spoke a great rationalist. Unfortunately, he did not stop in 1811, for by that time delusion was increasing its grip on his mind. As one Minister of the Empire remarked: 'It is strange that though Napoleon's common sense amounted to genius, he never could see where the possible left off. . . .' Here, if anywhere, lies one major clue to the ultimate disaster. Even his military talents declined in certain respects. There were still flashes of the old genius - as at the Beresina or in 1814 - but moral and physical bankruptcy warped his grand strategic judgment on a number of critical occasions.

As a military theorist, Napoleon was neither original nor revolutionary. His major contribution to the 'bless'd trade' lay in the executive aspect, the acid test for any commander. The gulf between precept and practice is immense, and a soldier's mastery of great strategic concepts is often less important than his ability to overcome the myriad practical difficulties encountered on a day-to-day basis, but Napoleon was highly skilled in both areas. At the root of his success lay 'an infinite capacity for taking pains' - one definition of genius - rather than immense original thought.

His largely undeserved reputation as a theoretical innovator springs from several sources. Napoleon was only too pleased to have his contemporaries believe him to be a unique military phenomenon - and through his propaganda set out sedulously to foster the image, both during his period of power and during the last years on St Helena. His main means to this end was steadfastly not to explain his methods in any great detail, or even in outline, thus fostering an illusion of sublime and unique abilities incapable of comprehension by ordinary mortals. During his locust years, it is notable that he never instituted a staff college or higher training institution for his more senior officers - an omission he came to regret after 1812 when his detached commanders, far from the master's comforting presence, were left very much on their own - a responsibility for which they were neither eager nor trained. Napoleon's reasons were, as ever, complex. If he liked to bask in a reputation of almost magical personal skill, he was also from first to last a wily opportunist. Aware that he had climbed to power by ruthless means, there was always that sneaking fear known to every dictator that he might one day be replaced by an able subordinate: he therefore saw little sense in imparting his innermost military secrets to men who might come to be his rivals.

His enemies were for many years quite prepared to be dazzled by Napoleon's mythical image as the super-general, for this at least helped excuse their own proven short-comings as commanders. Eventually, the Allies began to catch glimmerings of what Napoleon was about, and this enabled them to institute organisational reforms and to devise countermeasures which, added to the latter-day atrophy and distortion of Napoleon's ambitions and military systems, served ultimately to bring him down. Even then, their success left them surprised. A few foes, however, were capable of learning from their mistakes - and those of others - the Archduke Charles of Austria, General Gneisenau of Prussia and the great Duke of Wellington being of this select number. The last-named clearly discovered part of Napoleon's secret before he set out for the Peninsula in 1808, for he once spoke as follows:

> I have not seen them [the French] since the campaign in Flanders,
> when they were capital soldiers, and a dozen years of victory under
> Bonaparte must have made them better still. They have, besides, it
> seems, a new system of strategy which has out-manœuvred and
> overwhelmed all the armies of Europe...
>
> My die is cast, they may overwhelm me but I don't think they will
> out-manœuvre me. First, because I am not afraid of them, as
> everybody else seems to be; and secondly, because if what I hear of this
> system of manœuvre is true, I think it a false one as against steady
> troops. I suspect all the continental armies were more than half-beaten
> before the battle was begun - I, at least, will not be frightened
> beforehand.

Here we have several clues to the basic ingredients of Napoleonic
warfare. The Emperor's methods were based upon the
psychological domination of his opponents by keeping them
acutely apprehensive, bewildered and off-balance. This mental
conditioning was of great significance, and in many campaigns
before 1812 the foe was often more than half-beaten before the first
shot was exchanged. Napoleon deliberately exploited his charisma,
building up the myth of his invincibility.

To achieve this moral predominance, Napoleon invariably sought
to gain, and retain, the initiative. There are no truly defensive
campaigns by Napoleon before 1814, and even then he clearly
believed that 'the best form of defence was attack.' To gain the
initiative, Napoleon employed speed, deception and surprise to
mount *blitzkrieg* attacks of great energy. 'I may lose ground, but I
shall never lose a minute', he once claimed; or again, 'Ground we
may recover, time never.' These concepts involved very full and
detailed planning: maximum dispersal prior to battle (conversant
with security) was to be replaced by maximum concentration for
battle, and the apparently haphazard and opportunistic placing and
movement of French formations was in fact the product of much
careful staff-work. 'Whatever is not considered in depth is without
result.' Many campaign plans were under consideration months
before implementation - and even long before the declaration of
war. The fruit of these deliberations was a plan of infinite flexibility
and potential adaptation, capable of adjustment to suit the
thousand accidents and chances of active service. Here was
Napoleon's planning genius - the accurate estimation of all the

odds, the foreseeing of most likely problems, the making allowance for the wholly unforeseen or 'chance' developments - rather than the sudden flash of genius and inspiration. From first to last, Napoleon was a creature of painstaking habit and ruthless efficiency.

By 1803, and possibly from 1800 - he had one immense advantage to aid him. As early as 1796 he had stressed the primordial importance of true unity of command: 'Better one bad general than two good ones.' Once he was firmly in charge of the French state as well as of its armies, he was able to centralise and co-ordinate every aspect of the French war effort, and thus set the seal on the concept of 'the nation-in-arms'. As head of state, he alone decided policy or 'grand strategy' - selected objectives, decreed alliances, adopted or rejected plans. Next, as chief general of France, he dictated the strategies needed to carry out his aims and to co-ordinate the efforts of various armies, so that whether they were serving in Germany or Italy, in Poland or Spain, the various corps owed obedience to one ultimate authority - though problems of distance and high-level inexperience in quasi-independent command would ultimately prove the Achilles heel of the war effort. The Emperor similarly lost no chance to cajole further batches of conscripts and munitions out of the responsible governmental authorities, but badgered his ministers mercilessly. As senior commander in the field, he equally directed the 'grand tactics' - the day-to-day movements, broad plans of battle and disposition of reserves, which were equally vital ingredients of success. The only military field in which he did not actively intervene after 1799 was that of minor tactics - he left the details of fighting techniques to his subordinates, but again he made his preference for *l'ordre mixte* and massed batteries perfectly clear to one and all. In sum, Napoleon had a firm finger on every pulse of the French war machine, and though the system would ultimately develop grave weaknesses, this high degree of centralised authority, fully developed from 1804, was one major secret of his shattering success.

Napoleon's innate conservatism as a soldier can be illustrated by several telling examples. Many of his military concepts were drawn directly from his study of history and military affairs, and then improved upon and made to work by that ruthless, practical *daemon* which was the hall-mark of his genius. To the end of his life, he paid tribute to the seven commanders he believed great - Alexander, Hannibal, Caesar, Gustavus Adolphus, Turenne, Eugene and Frederick the Great. The last-named had a particular influence over him. Many of Napoleon's maxims and military sayings have parallels in Frederick's writings, and he freely borrowed (before transforming) Frederick's strategic concept of the 'central position', and adapted the 'oblique order' for part of his grand tactical system. Others who conditioned his thought were Guibert (the prophet of the nation-in-arms and near-total war), Bourcet, Turpin de Crissé, the Welshman Lloyd and the Chevalier de Folard. As for the theory and employment of artillery, he followed the work of Gribeauval as interpreted by the du Teil brothers.

If most of his military concepts were second-hand in their origin, so, too, did Napoleon distrust military innovations. He disbanded the balloon company formed during the Revolution, rejected Robert Fulton's offer of mines and rudimentary submarines and regarded other improvements with innate suspicion. On the other hand, one of his maxims runs: 'If it is feasible to make use of thunderbolts their use should be preferred to that of cannon.' The acid test was that of practicability.

Napoleon benefited greatly from the reforms introduced into the French Army following the humiliating defeats of the Seven Years' War in the mid-eighteenth century. Under the supervision of the Duc de Broglie, some effort was made to tackle the abuses associated with the purchase of commissions, and the development of experimental mixed divisions of all arms had been recommenced. Infantry tactics were also being reconsidered, the proponents of fighting in the traditional linear formations being challenged by the champions of the column. The outcome was the *ordre mixte*, whereby formations in column would be linked by others in line, thus combining the advantages of shock and fire action. The year 1777 had also seen the introduction of an improved flintlock musket, destined to remain in French service until the 1830s. Meanwhile, the whole art and science of

Lazare Carnot, 'the Organiser of Victory', was responsible for setting in train many of the reforms that transformed the French army from 1791 onwards. He served as Minister of War for many years and was regarded as being indispensable.

Jean-Mathieu-Philibert, Comte Sérurier (1742-1819). This Marshal was an aristocrat of l'Ancien Régime and a methodical soldier and severe disciplinarian rather than an inspired commander.

Alexandre Berthier, Marshal, Prince de Neuchâtel et Valangin, Prince de Wagram (1753-1815), Napoleon's indispensable Chief-of-Staff. He died mysteriously shortly before the Waterloo Campaign.

Louis Nicolas Davout, Marshal, Duc d'Eckmühl (1770-1823). One of Napoleon's ablest generals, he suffered slightly from his master's jealousy. He was also rather a dour character.

gunnery had been transformed by Gribeauval, who lightened the cannons by superior casting and design, improved trails and limbers, introduced interchangeable equipment and for field use standardised the calibres into four types - twelve, eight and four-pounders and six-inch howitzers. He also organised the guns into *compagnies* or batteries of eight pieces, and greatly improved the training schedules for artillery personnel. By the 1780s, these reforms were beginning to take effect, particularly in the artillery, and it was, of course, into that arm of the service that the young Bonaparte was commissioned. But it would be wrong to represent the situation as too favourable, for in other respects the forces of aristocratic, hide-bound conservatism remained strongly entrenched (even Broglie was forced into exile) and only the Revolution would affect the sweeping changes still required.

From 1792, the Revolution began to transform the French services. The disappearance of much of the officer corps - either purged or fled - caused some initial confusion in the infantry and cavalry, which early experiments in the election of new officers did little to improve. Only the artillery and engineers remained relatively unaffected by this development. Similarly, the large new-type volunteer armies of 1792 caused as many problems as they solved. Nevertheless, under the inspired leadership and guidance of Lazare Carnot, the 'organiser of victory', the Revolutionary armies managed to survive the perils of the first years of the war, and rapidly began to put their house in order. The most important developments of future significance were the following: a rudimentary general staff organisation made possible the higher control of the war effort, while the adoption of various measures leading to conscription (1798) provided a reservoir of soldiers making larger armies available. Dubois-Crancé implemented the universal adoption of all-arm divisions in 1794 - the vital step towards the formation of Napoleon's famous *corps d'armée* of later years.

Two other developments of the greatest significance were the concept of the 'nations-in-arms' - the wholesale mobilisation of the state's resources to support the war effort - and the extemporised doctrine of 'making war pay for war'. In the field of supply, this led to the adoption of the idea of requiring the troops to 'live off the countryside' for all save the most rudimentary rations. This approach came about by sheer necessity rather than deliberate design, for the support of the vastly increased numbers of troops sent to the frontiers at the crisis of the Revolution in 1792 was simply beyond the administrative machinery available at the time. Surprisingly, the new idea was found to work, at least in the relatively fertile and productive areas of Italy and central Europe, and the measure of increased mobility which the lack of reliance on huge convoys and pre-stocked magazines afforded the armies of Republican France would, under Napoleon, transform the conduct of campaigns.

The Revolution also produced, by natural selection, a whole class of leaders - Napoleon himself being, of course, the most conspicuous example. Early experiments with the election of officers proved unsatisfactory, but from 1793 promotion to even the highest ranks became based solely on talent (and political reliability). The proverbial bâton was 'in every soldier's knapsack' if he could prove his ability, and the very real prospects of advancement served as an invaluable inducement to valour and meritorious service. A number of Napoleon's future marshalate were already soldiers of distinction and officer rank under *l'Ancien Régime* - Berthier, Davout and Sérurier being among the most notable examples. Others were Sergeant-Majors or Non-

Commissioned Officers, including Massena, who earned rapid promotion during the Revolution. The 'career open to talent - the tools to him who can use them', as Carlyle wrote, became a reality, and resulted in a dynamic leadership of young men who would prove more than a match for the more experienced but generally older and more hidebound generals of their opponents.

Napoleon was also able to make use of, and to develop, the high morale of the French army. The average conscript of the French army tended to be more intelligent than his equivalent 'walking musket' in the older armies, and he demanded to know what he was fighting for. Once again, the Revolution provided ideological inspiration. Danton's famous declaration 'the Motherland in danger' served to rally national sentiment behind the tricolor in the desperate days of 1792, and the heady slogans of the Revolution, 'Liberté, Egalité, Fraternité' provided inspiration thereafter - as the soldiers became imbued with the idea that they were leading a worthy crusade to liberate the oppressed peoples of Europe from the control of reactionary regimes. As the years passed, these slogans would become a trifle worn-out and faded, but they would be replaced by an almost mystical reverence for the Emperor's person; his charisma would extend its magic over both officers and rank-and-file. As Wellington described it many years later, 'I used to say of him that his presence in the field was worth 40,000 men.'

Thus Napoleon was not called upon to create a new army from first principles or to reorganise his adopted country for war. The weapon was ready-forged - it required only fine tempering and then wielding with skill. He would improve the operation of many aspects of his war machine, adding a taste for la gloire through his skill at 'speaking to the soul' of the men whom he would lead all over Europe, and institute a system of rewards for outstanding service. For the rest, he would make the most devastating use of his resources. As has been well said, 'Napoleon gave nothing to the French army - except victory' - and, it is only fair to add, ultimate defeat.

Napoleon's operations from first to last, were directed towards short, decisive campaigns. Long-drawn-out wars of attrition (as in 1796, 1812 and 1813) were not to his liking, and were contrary to his military convictions. The quick destruction of the enemy's army was his basic formula for success. In his search for this victory he made his most original contribution to the art and science of war - by fusing marching, fighting and pursuing into one continuous process of war. There was no pause in a Napoleonic campaign. This

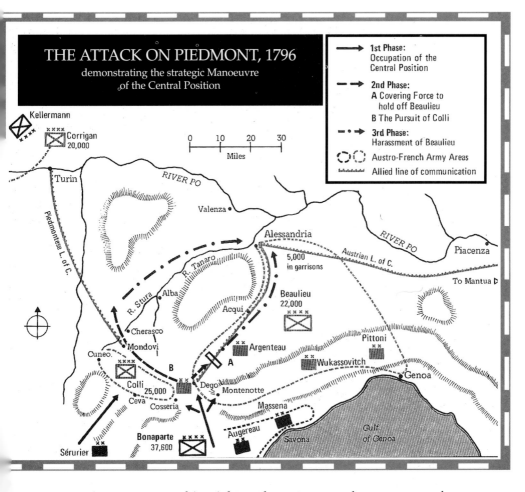

THE ATTACK ON PIEDMONT, 1796

demonstrating the strategic Manoeuvre of the Central Position

1st Phase: Occupation of the Central Position

2nd Phase:
A Covering Force to hold off Beaulieu
B The Pursuit of Colli

3rd Phase: Harassment of Beaulieu

Austro-French Army Areas

Allied line of communication

Kellermann

Corrigan 20,000

Turin

Piedmontese L. of C.

RIVER PO

Valenza

0   10   20   30

Miles

Alessandria

5,000 in garrisons

RIVER PO

Piacenza

Austrian L. of C.

To Mantua ▷

R. Tanaro

Alba

Acqui

R. Stura

Beaulieu 22,000

Cherasco

Mondovi

Cuneo

Argenteau

Pittoni

Wukassovitch

Genoa

B   A

Colli 25,000

Ceva

Cosseria

Dego

Montenotte

Massena

Bonaparte 37,600

Augereau

Savona

Gulf of Genoa

Sérurier

was in contrast to his eighteenth-century predecessors - and contemporary opponents - who marched in one formation and fought in another after time-consuming conversion.

Napoleon once claimed that he never employed a 'system of operations', but this statement was, at best, a half-truth. It is true that he was never dominated by a single plan or group of principles, for aspects of every campaign, operation and battle were unique. At the same time, however, the close study of the master's campaigns does reveal a number of basic underlying patterns or broad systems, and an understanding of the working of these is of central importance to any study of the campaigns.

At the level of strategy - the movement of forces to obtain a favourable battle situation - Napoleon employed three methods - either singly, or in combination. As before, they were not unique as concepts, but only in the way in which they were applied. First, and the least important, was the strategy of penetration, often employed at the opening of a campaign when a frontier's defences had to be pierced, or when a major obstacle, for instance a major defended river-line, had to be tackled by direct means. The French aims, using this method, were to induce the enemy to over-extend his forces into a long cordon by mounting feint or secondary attacks at otherwise irrelevant points, before achieving a crash concentration of force to make a decisive breakthrough at one selected point, giving the enemy scant chance to offer major opposition. Examples of this operation in use include the crossing of the River Mincio at Borghetto in late May 1796, and the crossing of the Niemen into Russia in June 1812. In every case, it was important to achieve surprise to enable bridges to be thrown across and a bridgehead developed on the farther bank ready to cover the transfer of the main forces. Penetration operations of this type could be very perilous if improperly prepared - as Napoleon learned to his cost at Aspern-Essling in 1809 when half his army became isolated over the River Danube in the presence of a powerful and aggressively-minded enemy army. On the other hand, the crossing of the Sambre at Charleroi on 15 June 1815 was a highly successful operation. This manœuvre frequently represented the opening gambit in a campaign, and was often associated with a more complex strategy based upon one or other of the two more important methods still to be described.

The second strategy often employed was that of the 'Central Position' which was commonly used when the French were faced by a superior opponent or series of opponents. Its aim, simply described, was to divide the enemy into several parts before achieving local superiority over each in turn and thus gaining a cumulative victory. For this purpose the French army was usually divided into four parts: an advance guard whose role, together with the cavalry screen, was to discover and occupy the 'central position', a left and right wing and a reserve. Both wings would attack the neighbouring enemy forces, generally at a numerical disadvantage, while the reserve would manœuvre to join one to build up a local superiority. If possible, part of the second wing would also be brought into the battle. Then, once the first enemy had been defeated, the reserve would march without delay to reinforce the second pinning force to gain a second success, leaving part of the victorious wing to pursue the original enemy.

This system was used, with variations, many times. Napoleon's first operation based on these ideas was the manœuvre of Montenotte and Ceva in April 1796 - shortly after he had taken over command of an army for the first time. The last was in June 1815, following the successful crossing of the Sambre already cited. On this one occasion, Napoleon revealed his strategic intention on paper for the benefit of Marshal Ney, commanding his left wing which was advancing to engage Wellington's Allied army while Grouchy (commanding the right wing) pressed back Blücher's leading corps of Prussians. 'For this campaign I have adopted the following general principle - to divide my army into two wings and a reserve: the Guard will form the reserve, and I shall bring it into action on either wing as circumstances may dictate. . . . Also, according to circumstances, I shall draw troops from one wing to strengthen my reserve.'

Of course, this method had its disadvantages. Even if successfully carried through, the outcome of the manúuvre would rarely be total victory, for at least one enemy force would survive to fight another day, as the French would not possess the strength to overwhelm both opponents, and timings were critical if the second foe were to be caught at a decisive disadvantage. Moreover, there was a straightforward counter-move for a discerning enemy; it might not prove possible to prevent his forces being divided, but at least he could strain every nerve to keep the various components within supporting distance of one another - even after a defeat. Thus, after Ligny on 16 June 1815, Blücher's army drew off north (partly by chance it is true) and thus kept within marching distance of Wellington, instead of retreating along its communications to the south-east, as Napoleon had assumed. As a result, Blücher was able to afford vital assistance at the crisis of the battle of Waterloo two days later. Nevertheless, the method achieved considerable successes for the French on many an earlier occasion.

Neither of the strategic methods outlined so far, however, was so important as the third - the manœuvre of envelopment. To be successful, this postulated a substantial French superiority of force, at least over the critical period, but in the event of success this strategy of the 'indirect approach' (as it can also be termed) could produce the total victory which was ever Napoleon's objective. The method was capable of infinite variation in detail, but its broad principles were as follows: At the opening of the campaign, a small but highly-integrated part of the French army would tempt the enemy army to make the first advance towards it. Once the enemy's attention had thus been forced on an objective, Napoleon would suddenly unleash his pre-positioned major force, and rush it by forced marches down the flank of the theatre of operations using any natural cover such as rivers, forests or a mountain range, supplemented by a screen of light cavalry operating in irrelevant as well as relevant areas to confuse the foe even more, with the intention of swinging a substantial force across the enemy's lines of communication far to the rear of his army. A lateral river-line with its bridges was the best strategic barrier to occupy for this purpose, as the enemy's reinforcements and supply convoys would inevitably be channelled to the available, and thus readily identifiable, crossings. Then, leaving sizable 'corps of observation' to seal off the sector and preclude the arrival of aid for the victim, the main force would advance towards the enemy army from its rear and seek out a promising battle position.

This type of blow was potentially devastating for psychological as well as physical reasons when employed against eighteenth-century-type armies and commanders in an age in which war fronts were not geographically continuous. Napoleon's blow was shrewdly intended to strike at the Achilles heel of such armies - their supply and administrative systems. All contemporary armies, save only the French, were dependent on the establishment of depots and magazines and the arrival of regular supply convoys at the front. To interrupt the flow of these supplies, and at the same time to sever the line of retreat, would compel many a foe to drop all further thought of advance in favour of a desperate retreat in an attempt to re-establish the lines of communication. The enemy was thus robbed of all initiative, and at the same time made psychologically uneasy. Moreover, waiting for the foe was the main French army in a pre-selected battle position ready to spring. In the event of the battle going successfully for the French, the enemy's position was likely to be almost impossible. Defeated, he had nowhere to go: the victorious French would still be blocking the line of retreat, and behind him the original French secondary force would be pressing forward to complete his discomfiture. This method, therefore, held the prospect of annihilation for the enemy: he was left with the choice between total destruction and surrender on the best terms obtainable.

This system was ideal for the new-type French army with its simplified logistical arrangements. Without complete reliance on waggon convoys, the corps could move fast and decisively. For the

General Mack surrenders his Austrian army at Ulm, 21 October 1805. This was the culmination of one of Napoleon's most successful 'manœuvres of envelopment' which induced the enemy to surrender without fighting a major battle.

same reasons, their own communications were nothing like so vulnerable or exposed as the enemy's, especially as Napoleon insisted that the rear lines of his army should be kept close to the front, and he was for ever establishing new centres of operations for his munitions and hospitals within three days' marching distance of the army, moving them forward regularly as the advance continued. Thus the enemy's nerve was likely to break before that of the French, and under such circumstances the foe was more than half-beaten before the first shot was exchanged.

This method, in varied form, Napoleon employed at least thirty times between 1796 and 1815. It was not always uniformly successful, of course, for many things could go wrong to spoil the effect, but on the other hand it brought off some astounding successes. First employed in the manœuvre of Lodi in May 1796, his system failed to achieve the destruction of the Austrian army on that occasion because the French timings were not perfect, and Beaulieu realised his danger just in time and slipped out of the trap - at the price of surrendering control over the Milanese. It also failed at Allenstein in 1807, when the Russian Bennigsen learned from a captured message what was afoot before the net had closed around him, while the atrocious Polish weather further hampered the French moves. On other occasions, too, the system had only part of the desired results - as at Smolensk in 1812. Nevertheless, the major successes represented by the great campaigns of 1800, when Napoleon swept over the Alps to confront Melas in north Italy, using a French force bottled-up in Genoa as the bait, or the first part of that of 1805* when Murat distracted Mack's attention while Napoleon swept from the Rhine to the Danube to encircle Ulm from the rear and induced the enemy to capitulate without a major battle, demonstrate the potential of the concept. So does the campaign of 1806, when Napoleon distracted the Prussians by having his brother Louis mount demonstrations towards Hamburg from the Rhine while the mass of the *Grande Armée* traversed the defiles of the Franconian Forest to penetrate deep into Saxony, there ultimately to find a great double-victory at Jena-Auerstadt. The system would also have later successes, including the manœuvre of Friedland and that of Bautzen in 1807 and 1813 respectively.

Once again, however, there were effective counters available once the enemy had learned what to expect at the hands of Napoleon and his armies. A decade of defeat taught some hard lessons, but these were assimilated, and once Napoleon became more predictable much of the hypnotic effect of his devastating manœuvres began to wear off. To call Napoleon's bluff (for that, after all, was what lay at the base of the system) required the massing of large quantities of ready-use supplies immediately behind the army - to lessen the practical effects of Napoleon's appearance in the more distant rear - and a steady determination to press ahead against the smaller French force to the fore and the targets beyond - leaving the French to do their worst in the rear. Thus, Blücher aborted Napoleon's rush up the River Mulde to attack his rear before Leipzig in 1813, and the following year the Allies called the Emperor's bluff for the last time by ignoring his seizure of St Dizier and pressing ahead for the ultimate goal of Paris. They became aware that the secret of success was to avoid Napoleon in person and to concentrate on his lieutenants and thus rob him of initiative and control by compelling him to repair the damage inflicted on his outlying detachments. Nevertheless, if Napoleon does stand accused of becoming predictable and lacking originality, there is equally no denying the fifteen years of triumph which his methods afforded him.

* See map page 64.

It would be erroneous to claim that each campaign held only one of these manœuvres at its base, for Napoleonic warfare was highly complex, an ever-shifting kaleidoscope of moves and intentions which as often as not left the foe completely bewildered. Thus, one strategic manœuvre often led into another of a different type.

The Italian campaign of 1796 started on the Ligurian coast as a manœuvre based on the 'central position' designed to separate the Piedmontese and Austrians, developed into a 'strategy of envelopment' in the Po valley, became a 'strategic penetration' on the River Mincio and was then transformed into a whole series of manœuvres based upon the 'central position' to defeat successive Austrian attempts to relieve Manuta. Similar patterns are equally detectable in later campaigns.

Napoleon's strategy would not have worked had his grand tactics and organisation not complemented his overall designs. The concept of the 'strategic battle' was one of Napoleon's most telling contributions to the art and science of warfare.

His fusion of manœuvre, battle and pursuit into one devastating process has already been mentioned, and the strategic battle was the climax of the process. 'It is often in the system of campaign that one conceives the system of battle', he once wrote, and there was often a close similarity between the grand tactical plan of a number of major battles and the 'strategy of envelopment' and that of the 'central position'. This is what made the fusion of marching and fighting a reality.

Before describing these combinations, it is important to examine the means that made possible both the strategies and the battles. Both were built on the *corps d'armée* organisation and the Napoleonic doctrine of 'concentration and dispersal'.

The *corps d'armée* grew out of the experiments of de Saxe, de Broglie and Dubois-Crancé. It was the descendent of the 'legion' of 1745, the 'grand divisions' of the 1770s and the 'mixed divisions' of the Revolution.

It was not a Napoleonic idea as such - though he fostered and expanded its development to the logical limits - and the first real corps per se were those employed by General Moreau in Germany in 1800. However, on occasions, Napoleon had made use of ad hoc groups of divisions in both 1796 and 1800 in north Italy, but his ideas on the subject came to full practical fruition only between 1803 and 1805.

In the simplest terms, a *corps d'armée* was a miniature army, containing elements of infantry, cavalry and artillery besides

Smolensk, 1812, was the scene of a two-day battle that ended inconclusively. Shortly afterwards, Napoleon took one of his most vital decisions - to press on for Moscow.

medical and supply services, together with a staff. Their command was generally entrusted to a senior general, or, from 1804, to a marshal. In size they varied enormously, some comprising barely fifteen thousand men, others as many as thirty thousand or even more - depending upon the intended role of the formation and the Emperor's estimation of the capabilities of the commander. Their composition often fluctuated even in mid-campaign or on the very eve of battle, as Napoleon would move a division from this corps to that, or even create a completely new formation from transferred components, as his restless mind devised subtle solutions to strategic problems. This fluidity or flexibility of the system was a feature which time and again hopelessly confused enemy intelligence as it tried to assess French strengths and intentions.

In addition to this quality of unsettling the enemy intelligence, the corps afforded Napoleon a number of other important advantages and opportunities. Perhaps the most important of all was the fact that a corps, a miniature army, was capable of fighting alone for a considerable period against considerably superior enemy forces until help could be brought its way. Napoleon wrote to his stepson, Eugène, in 1809:

Here is the general principle of war - a corps of 25,000-30,000 men can be left on its own. Well handled, it can fight or alternatively avoid action, and manœuvre according to circumstances without any harm coming to it, because an opponent cannot force it to accept an engagement, but if it chooses to do so it can fight alone for a long time. A division of 9,000-17,000 men can be left for an hour on its own without inconvenience; it will contain a foe several times more numerous than itself, and will win time for the arrival of the army.

This ability to take on substantial odds without courting complete destruction, providing assistance could be brought up within the time limit, had another important implication. Under these circumstances, a corps could be safely routed through the countryside along its own axis of advance. This ability often increased both overall range and mobility - the available roads would be reserved for the use of only a single major formation in any one sector; moreover, this also assisted 'living off the countryside' as each corps would be provided with its own area of subsistence. Thus, the French army habitually moved over large distances in a web of scattered (but carefully co-ordinated) *corps d'armée* - as in the great sweep from the Rhine to the Danube in 1805 - which could completely fox the enemy concerning ultimate French intentions as reports would arrive from every quarter indicating enemy columns on the march towards unspecified objectives. These characteristics of mobility, subsistence and security, were advantages which old-fashioned armies, moving along a single set of roads in a narrow area, unit behind unit, could never enjoy. Equally important, the system often enabled the Emperor to leave open his strategic and tactical options until the

General Moreau, an able French general of the Revolutionary and Consulate period, who constituted the only possible rival to Napoleon as a soldier. He was banished in 1803 after suspected complicity in a royalist plot, later served on the staff of Allied armies, and was present at Leipzig.

last possible moment. The secret was to ensure that each corps was always within twenty-four hours' marching distance of one or more of it neighbours, and within thirty-six to forty-eight hours' march of the greater part of the army, so that any particular formation could be reinforced, or diverted elsewhere as a reinforcement, as circumstances might dictate.

This organisation reached perhaps its ultimate refinement in 1806 in the *battalion carré* which swept into Saxony. Operating in a vast diamond-shape of formations, the French army proved capable of changing its direction of march from north to west with the minimum of delay and dislocation. All this was made possible by the flexibility and fighting-capacity of the individual *corps d'armée,* which may be said to constitute the French secret weapon of the Napoleonic Wars.

The corps system lay at the basis of Napoleon's tenet concerning 'marching dispersed but concentrating for battle'. The wider the strategic web of corps could be spread, the more likely was a contact with the enemy. Once this had been established, every unit would 'march on the sound of the guns' to join their embattled colleagues in a full trial of strength. By the term 'assembly' of an army, Napoleon meant the placing of sufficient forces within range of the battlefield, but not necessarily within sight of it. This was replaced by 'concentration' of force as the crisis approached and time and again Napoleon proved able to produce far more men on the battlefield - as at Austerlitz or Bautzen - than the enemy ever anticipated.

Napoleon's plans for fighting battles were, of course, varied. No two were exactly the same, but they fit into three broad patterns or types. The straightforward battle of attrition, with the two armies facing up to one another on equal fronts, with their respective lines of communication stretching away behind them, he liked least (as for example, at Borodino). The second type was the 'double-battle', when the Emperor would designate a double struggle, as at Quatre Bras and Ligny on 16 June 1815, or would find himself unexpectedly committed to one - as at Jena-Auerstädt in October 1806. His favourite form of grand tactics was the 'strategic battle' - which promised near-total success if it was controlled with sufficient skill. He once likened this type of engagement - which he only rarely managed to bring off - to a *pièce de théâtre* 'of several acts', each leading on to the next.

The sequence of a strategic battle was as follows. As the French corps, preceded by their cavalry, scoured the country seeking out the enemy, news would reach headquarters that one part of the army had at last found the foe. The standard order for the formation that ran into the enemy was to engage, heedless of odds, and then alert headquarters and neighbouring corps, providing them with a fixed point upon which to march. The neighbouring corps would march to its assistance, thus escalating the struggle, while the Emperor decided upon the form of his grand tactical plan. Once he had learned from his screen of scouting cavalry the direction in which the foe's lines of communication were running, he would often order part of his uncommitted forces to march by a circuitous route to place itself - secretly - in a position near the flank and rear of the enemy army close to the roads in question. There it would lie concealed for the present.

Meanwhile, the remainder of the reserve - cuirassiers, horse artillery and the Guard - would be brought up by forced marches to mass (unnoticed if possible) behind the French front opposite the threatened enemy flank. These moves would constitute the 'second act' of the battle drama.

The frontal battle would grow in intensity with the intention of drawing into action as many enemy reserves as possible. Once this process was sufficiently advanced, Napoleon would order the concealed corps to make its presence known as the third phase began. Alarmed by the sudden appearance of a considerable force threatening his line of retreat, the enemy - if sufficiently pinned by the actions already raging - would be compelled to find a force to meet the new threat. If Napoleon's timing and calculations were correct (and the matter of timing was of the very essence), this could be done only by weakening the sector nearest to the danger.

Then, having allowed sufficient time to elapse for these re-
deployments to take effect, Napoleon would unleash his reserves -
ready-massed opposite the weakened sector - pass them through
the front and mount a devastating attack with battle-fresh troops,
preceded by a hurricane of shot from the massed artillery.

If a breakthrough were achieved, a gap would be made through
the enemy's front - and into it would pour the massed squadrons of
French light cavalry, sweeping into the enemy's rear, converting
defeat into disaster and heading the immediate pursuit of the
survivors as the typically ruthless Napoleonic exploitation was put
into operation.

Such was the theoretical sequence of a Napoleonic 'strategic
battle'. It was rare for an engagement to follow these lines exactly,
as many complications could obviously arise, but Napoleon first
attempted such an engagement at Castiglione in August 1796,
based Friedland upon the scheme in June 1807 and certainly fought
Bautzen by this method in 1813. Marengo, too, as fought, held many
equivalent features, and helped Napoleon to develop his concept. It
would be too bold to claim that his battles were always planned
along these lines, but the basic method was often present in his
mind.

The Emperor's interest in minor tactics was limited, and as often
as not after 1800 he left tactical matters to his subordinates.
However, we do know his preference for massed batteries, for
l'ordre mixte of column and line, and his insistence on the proper co-
ordination of all-arm attacks. In Egypt, in 1798, he personally
devised a drill for the formation of massive divisional squares of the
type employed at the battle of the Pyramids against the hordes of
Mameluke horsemen. He was convinced also of the all-importance
of the attack being pressed home with the greatest élan, providing it
proceeded from a sound defensive base which could sustain it in
case of repulse or failure. He also believed that cannon were the
main instruments of fire-power, preferring the sabre or bayonet-
charge as shock weapons for cavalry and infantry.

The evolution of French tactics and organisations between 1792
and 1815 was partly haphazard and partly deliberate. In the early
days of Valmy, the problem of making effective use of the unskilled
fédérés - as often as not half-starved, under-equipped and semi-
mutinous - had encouraged the amalgamation of two unskilled
with every one experienced formation. The former mounted mass
attacks in crude columns of attack, while the latter provided the
light infantry screen and musketry fire-support, drawn up in line.

Cavalry of 'La Grande Armée'

Behind all Napoleon's achievements stood la grande armée, the instrument of military glory and the indispensable weapon of conquest. Imbued with an almost fanatical adoration for 'le Tondu' (literally 'the shorn-one', the Guards' nickname for Napoleon referring to his preference after 1800 for short hair, cut 'à la Titus'), his troops would suffer any hardship or danger for him and they did, right to the end.

Right: The light cavalry, the 'darlings of the ladies' are represented by a dashing hussar, whose splendid uniforms were based upon Hungarian models. Their campaign roles were chiefly reconnaissance, patrolling and pursuit.

Below: A French cuirassier fighting with a British Life Guard at Waterloo; the heavy cavalry were supposed to weigh 16 stone apiece, and still wore body-armour in action.

The popular woodcut depicts several types of cavalry, both French and German, alleged to have been present at the battle of Jena. It is rather unlikely, however, that Russian 'cossacks' were present - although Prussian Uhlans may well have been.

This was, of course, an adaptation of Guibert's *ordre mixte*. Under the Revolutionary requirements, the old regiments were replaced by three-battalion *demi-brigades,* which in action combined the functions of shock and fire action as already indicated. The cavalry of the Revolution was probably the weakest part of the army, being the worst hit by the flight of officers and needing the longest time to recruit and train, and at the same time the artillery was indubitably the most professional and effective arm of the service. The guns silenced their opponents, then supported the French attacks; the cavalry did its best to check the enemy horsemen, and to exploit success when achieved.

Over the years, the organisation of French formations changed considerably. The infantry battalion of the Revolution originally comprised three companies of 330 men apiece; before 1800, however, the number of companies had been raised to nine (including one grenadier company) of between 150 and 200 men each. Between 1805 and 1808, a simplification took place, the number of companies being reduced to six (including one of grenadiers and one of *voltigeurs* or light infantry). From 1803 the regiment was reintroduced in place of the *demi-brigade.* The growing popularity of light infantry led to the formations of numerous units. In 1803 there were ninety line and twenty-six light regiments, and by 1813 there was a total of 243 formations, one-sixth of them light infantry.

The infantry column of attack was often organised on a two-company frontage, a formation perhaps fifty to seventy-five men wide and twelve ranks deep. A battalion in line drew up three ranks deep. Combinations of the two made the most of fire-power and shock action - bullets and bayonets, and adaptations of *l'ordre mixte* were employed up to divisional level. On occasions, attack columns would be formed on a single-company frontage - for an attack up a defile or other restricted area. In theory, columns were supposed to deploy into line some 150 yards from the enemy, but in practice they often charged home without pausing to re-form. The light infantry formations were habitually deployed as a screen ahead of the columns, sniping at individual targets.

Such commanders as the younger Kellermann, Grouchy, Lasalle and, above all, Murat, rapidly transformed the cavalry. Each cavalry *demi-brigade* (later regiment) comprised four squadrons of two *compagnies* (or troops) apiece, each holding up to 116 cavalrymen. There were three categories of cavalry. The heavies, or cuirassiers and carabiniers, eventually comprised seventeen

The bearers of the brunt of almost every battle, les fantassins, or infantry, shown here storming a battery position. Note the light infantry bugle-horn in the left foreground.

regiments of 1,040 troopers apiece, and became increasingly retained for service in the Reserve Cavalry, used for critical breakthroughs, organised into divisions. Secondly there were up to thirty regiments of dragoons, each with five squadrons and a total of 1,200 men. They usually fought on horseback, but could, exceptionally, be employed on foot, each man being armed with a dragoon musket as well as sword and pistols. Thirdly there was the light cavalry - hussars, chasseurs-à-cheval, light horse (later lancers) and the like, the darlings of the ladies - to a total of over thirty regiments, many of which contained up to five squadrons or eighteen hundred sabres apiece. These dashing horsemen habitually formed the cavalry screen and performed many reconnaissance as well as battle duties. All cavalry were trained to

*A grenadier of the Imperial Guard, the archetypal 'grognard' or 'grumbler' -
Napoleon's nickname for his men - wearing campaign dress. A slouch-hat was
often worn instead of the bearskin, at least for marching. His soldiers may
have grumbled, but they would follow Napoleon to the furthermost parts of
Europe and the Orient.*

Napoleon én bivouac during the night 5-6 July 1809, at Wagram, surrounded by members of his 'Little', or battle, headquarters staff. His gift for cat-napping, whether by day or night, made possible sustained periods of hectic activity when circumstances demanded it.

perform a variety of evolutions, including of course the charge, a carefully-graduated advance which progressively picked up speed as the target became closer. They were also trained to exploit success to the uttermost, the need to rally being stressed.

The artillery was divided into two main types - horse and foot. Organised into *compagnies* (or batteries) of eight guns and howitzers apiece, the number of horse artillery batteries grew rapidly. In 1800 there were eight regiments of foot artillery to six of horse, and the number grew a little though the usual practice was to create additional batteries for already existing regiments rather than to raise new regiments. Brigaded with the *compagnies* were the *pontonniers* or bridging trains, and battalions of artillery train troops (eight by 1800). In 1805 France possessed a total of over twenty thousand cannon, howitzers and mortars, and by 1813 artillery personnel numbered all of 103,000 men. Artillery tactics were based upon rapid fire (up to five rounds a minute) and the progressive advance to almost point-blank range of the enemy in a series of bounds. The heavier guns - twelve-pounders - were often massed in large batteries from 1806 onwards, and as the quality of the French infantry deteriorated, so were more guns added at regimental and divisional level. Formations of horse artillery and *artillerie volante* (galloper-guns), together with a proportion of twelve-pounders, were invariably kept in army reserve under Napoleon's personal control, for use in special tasks. The most experienced artillery generals - after the Emperor himself - included Marmont and Drouot. The guns fired round-shot and case or canister, while howitzers fired shells as well as canister, and mortars (mostly employed against buildings) fired bombs. There were also, of course, massive fortress guns which never took the field with the armies.

Special mention must be made of the Imperial Guard. Originating from the Guards of the Directory and the Guides (or escort) of the Army of Italy, the Consular Guard of 1799 became the Imperial Guard in 1804, when it comprised 4,000 grenadiers, 2,000 *élite* cavalry and twenty-four guns. By mid-1805 it had grown to over 12,000 men, by 1812 it numbered all of 60,000, and in 1814 no less than 112,500 soldiers could claim some form of membership of the Guard - an immense and much-sought honour which carried privileges of pay and treatment as well as of prestige. The original nucleus became known as the Old Guard. In 1806 the Middle Guard was formed (eventually four regiments strong), and in 1809 the Young Guard came into existence. The first two formations were recruited from the veterans of the army; the last-mentioned from the cream of the annual conscript classes. The draining-off of the most experienced soldiers and NCOs into the Guard was of questionable value in its effect on the line formations thus deprived of their best men, but there is no doubt that the charisma of the Guard was a factor of importance on many a battlefield, second only to that of Napoleon himself. Until 1812, the Emperor proved reluctant to use this *élite* force in action, but in the last years it was frequently sent in, especially in 1813 and 1814. The Imperial Guard comprised horse, foot and guns - and thus was in effect, in its later years, a miniature army. Standards, save possibly in the Young Guard, were maintained from first to last.

Napoleon's use of the power at his disposal can best be illustrated by a typical sequence of events. On most occasions, the French were determined to seize the initiative and attack. First, the massive 'battery of position' would be established, and open fire. Its heavy bombardment was designed to shake enemy morale and inflict as much damage as possible on his most exposed formations. Under cover of the fire, swarms of light infantry would advance in open order to within musketry range, and add a disconcerting nuisance value by sniping at officers or gunners.

After this 'softening-up', a series of heavy cavalry and infantry attacks would be launched. The secret of these was careful timing and co-ordination. As the light infantry drew aside, the massed squadrons of horsemen thundered past to defeat the enemy cavalry and then, if all was going well, proceeded to attack the serried ranks of infantry drawn up beyond. These charges were designed to force the regiments to form square rather than to achieve an immediate breakthrough. Although infantry squares were rarely broken by cavalry attack, provided the men remained cool and steady, they presented good targets for the batteries of French horse artillery which accompanied the cavalry, and proceeded to unlimber and go into devastating action at near point-blank range.

All this frenzied activity was designed to facilitate the main attack, entrusted to the hurrying columns of infantry moving up from the rear. If the infantry attack was properly timed, the columns and their supporting battalions drawn up in line for fire action would be close to the enemy lines before the French cavalry drew off, to re-form.

Ideally, the French columns would catch the enemy still in square - a formation which obviously greatly reduced the amount of fire-power that could be brought to bear against the new menace. By this time, the excitement and enthusiasm of the columns would have become intense, and after a few scattered volleys they would hurl themselves upon their weary opponents and as often as not rout them.

This was the moment for the reserves to move up and exploit the break-in - fresh columns and horse-artillery batteries forming and widening the walls of the corridor being driven into the enemy line of battle. Into and through this salient would come the massed French light cavalry, reserved for this moment, their sabres rising and falling relentlessly as they fell upon the last islands of enemy resistance, their effect being to convert local defeat into full-scale rout.

Such was one possible tactical battle of a French *corps d'armée*. A whole series of similar blows would be being mounted against different sectors of the enemy battle-line - with variations according to the grand tactical plan, and the cumulative effect of such pressure could be devastating to all but the stoutest and most experienced foe.

Only when the enemy began to use similar formations and tactical concepts did these methods begin to become less effective - as in the Peninsula, where the combination of Wellington's skill at selecting concealed battlegrounds, the general dearth of sufficient cavalry owing to the inhospitable nature of much of the Spanish terrain, his use of deployed Riflemen on the forward slopes to gain time, and the devastating effect of reserved fire by highly-disciplined battalions drawn-up in protected reverse-slope position, all served to thwart the French onslaughts and turn them back in red ruin, as often as not concerted into rout by a determined bayonet charge. Nevertheless, the methods described brought the French almost a decade of unrivalled success elsewhere.

To complete this survey of Napoleon's methods of war, we must examine the nerve-centre that directed this impressive war machine, the *Grande Armée*. The direction, administration and co-ordination of forces that eventually numbered more than half a million men was a daunting task in the days before radio or telegraphy, and the fact that there were many deficiencies of control is less amazing than that the system worked at all, given the rudimentary means of communication available to armies of the period. Lazare Carnot, as we have had occasion to mention, had created the nucleus of a rudimentary General Staff organisation in his *Bureau Topographique*. The Ministries of War and Marine were situated in Paris, but their activities were taken up mainly with the administration of the Conscription Laws together with the equipment, supply and movement of men and the over-all logistical support of the forces, rather than with matters of policy; for, from first to last, Napoleon kept the tightest personal control over the strategic direction of France's wars, on both land and sea, so that from 1804 for all practical purposes his Imperial Headquarters, or *Grand-Quartier-Général* was the supreme authority for the issue of his directives, at least in time of active war.

Le Grand-Quartier-Général expanded over the years from some 250 officers and men to the size of a small army corps by 1812. In its heyday it comprised three main sections: the Maison, Napoleon's personal headquarters; the General Headquarters - the responsibility of Marshal Berthier, Chief of Staff; and the general administrative headquarters, under the *Intendant,* for some time the province of Count Daru.

The *Maison* was by far the most important; through it Napoleon ruled France as well as directed the campaigns. It was divided into two main, and a number of subsidiary parts. The true never-centre, the 'sanctuary of genius' as it has been well called, was the Emperor's Cabinet, including the *Bureau Topographique* or map-office. This was small in size - a few dozen key advisers, including civilians, of whom the most important after Berthier (who was *ex-officio* member of both sections of the General Staff) was the obscure General Bacler l'Albe with whom Napoleon conducted his twice-daily planning sessions. Secondly there was the Emperor's personal household - the officers, officials and servants responsible for his personal well-being and service under the general supervision of the Marshal-of-the-Palace, Duroc, and including a considerable number of general officers serving as *aides-de-camp*. There would also be attendant staffs provided by the key Ministries in Paris - the

Treasury, the Ministry of Foreign Affairs and the military Ministries. In 1812, when the staff reached its largest proportions, some of these institutions were kept well in the rear - that of Foreign Affairs for instance never moving farther forward than Vilna hard by the Russo-Polish frontier.

The General Headquarters was sub-divided into several branches, and performed much of the routine day-to-day running of the army. Berthier controlled four major sub-sections or *Bureaux*. First of these was the Chief of Staff's own Cabinet, roughly equivalent to Napoleon's own, which was particularly concerned with troop movements and all matters of military intelligence. The second *Bureau* was responsible for records and personnel - including the maintenance of the daily *cahiers* which detailed the fighting strength of every formation. The third busied itself with matters pertaining to legal matters, including prisoners-of-war and deserters. The fourth was responsible for headquarters administration, including its quartering, maintenance and movement, not to forget its security. The Guard, Artillery and Engineers also ran staff organisations.

The administrative headquarters often functioned well to the rear, and contained numbers of departments specialising in munitions, convoys and other aspects of logistical support, including the setting up and administration of the successive *centres d'opérations* that were established in the wake of the main army.

For operational purposes, the Emperor was accompanied on inspections or the field of battle by his 'little headquarters'. This usually comprised Berthier, General Caulaincourt (the Grand Equerry and Master of the Horse), the Marshal-of-the-day on duty, a couple of aides-de-camp, twice as many orderly officers, one page (entrusted with Napoleon's telescope), his Mameluke bodyguard, Roustam, a groom, an officer-interpreter and a soldier of the escort carrying the map portfolio. Four squadrons of Guard Cavalry habitually formed the escort under command of a general. For normal journeys, Napoleon would ride carefully-trained Arab horses, of whom 'Marengo' was the most famous, but for longer distances he would transfer to his *calèche* or his post-chaise, which was in effect a mobile office.

Such then, was the outline of the French *Grand-Quartier-Général*. Equivalent staffs, on a progressively smaller scale, existed at *corps d'armée* and divisional levels. On the whole, the system functioned reasonably well until 1812, when the problems of time and space became almost unsurmountable. The staff organisation was in some ways top-heavy and inadequate, with curious over-laps of function and design which did nothing to improve its performance. Nevertheless, it was the most sophisticated general staff system in Europe until the Prussian reforms of the post-1807 period, which in due course developed the prototype of all modern staffs with the three main branches - General, Adjutant-General and Quartermaster-General.

All in all, the French army became a formidable weapon for Napoleon's limitless ambitions, as, indeed, did the French nation he ruled. Napoleon's was a heroic career which for good or evil - the balanced view would say both - transformed the continent which he dominated for so long. The implications of his achievements were profound, casting their shadow far into succeeding generations and leaving the Napoleonic legend itself to be debated by successive schools of historians alternatively captivated or repelled by the sheer scale of his influence. Napoleon is not to be judged solely as a commander, or as a national leader, or even as a man. He was one of those few men whose lives have to be seen as part of history itself, shaping and shaped by the evolution of nations, societies and ideas. If it dazzles the historian in retrospect, we may imagine Napoleon's impact on contemporaries who witnessed at first hand the brilliance of his rise, the finality of his eclipse, the birth and death of that star which guided, in his belief, his future and his destiny.

Select Bibliography

Of books on Napoleon and his period there is no end, but the selection that follows represents a reasonable 'working library'. Many, including the author's *The Campaigns of Napoleon* (The Macmillan Company, New York, 1966) include full bibliographies for the guidance of the serious student. Here many memoirs and specialist works are not mentioned, but reputable secondary authorities are listed, with a leavening of primary sources.

Adye, Sir J., *Napoleon of the Snows*, London 1931.
Aubry, O., *Napoléon*, Paris 1964.
Bainville, J., *Napoleon*, London 1932.
Becke, A.F., *Napoleon and Waterloo*, London 1939.
Belloc, H., *Napoleon*, London 1932.
Brett-James, A., *The Hundred Days*, London 1964.
Camon, H., *Génie et métier chez-Napoléon*, Paris 1929.
Carlyel, T., *Critical and Miscellaneous Essays*, London 1843.
Caulaincourt, A., *Memoirs*, London 1950.
Clausewitz, K.von, *On War*, London 1909.
Coignet, J., *The Notebooks of Captain Coignet*, ed. J. Fortescue, London 1929.
Colin, J., *The Transformations of War*, London 1912.
Cronin, V., *Napoleon*, London 1971.
Delderfield, E., *The March of the Twenty-Six*, London 1962.
Dodge, T., *Napoleon*, New York 1904.
Duffy, C.J., *Borodino*, London 1972.
Dupont, M., *Napoléon et ses Grognards*, Paris 1945.
Esposito, V. & Elting, J., *A Military History and Atlas of the Napoleonic Wars*, New York 1964.
Faber du Four, C., *La Campagne de Russie, 1812*, Paris 1895.
Fain, A., *Mémoires*, Paris 1884.
Fisher, H., *Napoleon*, London 1950.
Fuller, J., *The Decisive Battles of the Western World*, London 1956.
Geyl, P., *Napoleon, For and Against*, London 1946.
Herold, C., *The Age of Napoleon*, New York 1963.
Hudson, W., *The Man, Napoleon*, London 1915.
Jackson, W., *Attack in the West*, London 1953.
Jomini, A., *The Art of War*, Philadelphia 1875.
Lachouque, H., *The Anatomy of Glory*, London and New York 1961.

Las Cases, E., *Memoirs of the Emperor Napoleon*, London 1836.
Lecestre, L., *Lettres inédites de Napoléon Iier*, Paris 1897.
Liddell-Hart, B., *The Ghost of Napoleon*, London 1933.
MacDonnell, A., *Napoleon and his Marshals*, London 1950.
Manceron, C., *Austerlitz*, Paris 1962.
Marbot, M., *Mémoires*, Paris 1962.
Markham, F., *Napoleon*, London 1963.
Marshall-Cornwall, Sir J., *Napoleon*, London 1967.
Napoléon Iier, *Correspondence*, Paris 1858-70.
Odeleben, E.d', *Relation de la Campagne de 1813*, Paris 1817.
Petre, F., *Napoleon's Conquest of Prussia*, London 1972.
Phipps, R., *The Armies of the First French Republic*, Oxford 1935-9.
Quimby, R., *The Background of Napoleonic Warfare*, New York 1957.
Rose, J., *Life of Napoleon*, London 1902.
Thompson, J., *Life of Napoleon*, Oxford 1952.
Vachée, A., *Napoleon at Work*, London 1914.
Wartenburg, Y.von, *Napoleon as a General*, London 1902.
Wilkinson, S., *The Rise of General Bonaparte*, Oxford 1930.
Young, P., *Napoleon's Marshals*, Reading 1973.

Acknowledgements

Picture researchers were Mathilde Rieussec in Paris and Michele Mason in London.

The general maps were drawn by Design Practitioners Ltd from those printed in *The Campaigns of Napoleon* by David G Chandler, and published by The Macmillan Company, New York, 1966. The originals were drawn by Sheila Waters from preliminary drafts prepared by the author. Battle sketch diagrams were also drawn by Design Practitioners Ltd, in part from references originally published in *Summaries of Selected Military Campaigns*, 1961 and produced by the Department of Military Art and Engineering, United States Military Academy, West Point, New York.

Index